The Employment Law Checklist

Sixth Edition

by

Erich Suter
BA, MIOSH, FIPM
of the Middle Temple, Barrister

Principal, Industrial Relations Workshop
IPD's Employment Law Adviser

Institute of Personnel and Development

First published 1981 as *Legislation for Personnel Managers: A checklist*

Reprinted 1982; revised 2nd edition 1982; revised 3rd edition 1985; revised 4th edition 1990; revised 5th edition 1992; revised 6th edition 1997.

Phototypeset by Fakenham Photosetting Ltd, Fakenham, Norfolk.
Printed in Great Britain by
The Short Run Press, Exeter

British Library Cataloguing in Publication Data
A catalogue record for this book is available from the British Library

ISBN 0–85292–679–0

The views expressed in this book are the author's own and may not necessarily reflect those of the IPD.

INSTITUTE OF PERSONNEL
AND DEVELOPMENT

IPD House, Camp Road, London SW19 4UX
Tel: 0181 971 9000   Fax: 0181 263 3333
Registered office as above. Registered Charity No. 1038333
A company limited by guarantee. Registered in England No. 2931892

Contents

Part 3
Recommended reading   **152**

Introduction

This edition of *The Employment Law Checklist* revises and updates previous editions, the last of which was published in 1992. On this occasion it is not just new law which has caused changes, but a mass of consolidating legislation. In all the major areas covered by this work there have been consolidations of the law. The coverage of the work has also been extended to include a number of statutory regulations which are of particular importance, ranging from the 'six-pack' regulations on health and safety and regulations on health and safety representation, through regulations requiring consultation in redundancy and transfer of undertakings situations in non-unionised employments and regulations taking away the erstwhile statutory maximum awards in discrimination cases to regulations which alter the scope of industrial tribunal jurisdiction and procedure. In all, 24 statutes and 13 sets of statutory regulations are added in this edition of the checklist. It should be borne in mind that this book is, and is intended to be, no more than a 'thumbnail' guide to employment legislation. Much of the statutory material covering employment matters, eg health and safety at work, is contained in statutory instruments and other delegated legislation, supported by codes of practice. Even with the increased coverage of regulations in this edition, much of the material which is dealt with in Regulations and which is often specific to a very small part of industry, has not been included. Apart from delegated legislation, a considerable part of the law surrounding employment has not been codified into Acts of Parliament and many fundamental parts of the law (eg contract, negligence, etc.) remain the province of the common law (or 'judge-made law'). For the above reasons, readers should rely on this guide merely as a starting point to ensure that they are aware of the more basic requirements of the law relating to employment and to update their knowledge of those requirements. Those with specific legal problems are recommended to take professional legal advice.*

The 'new format' for the checklist (first adopted for the 4th edition in 1990) has been maintained and the layout is as follows:

1. Chronological list of legislation – lists in date order all the legislation detailed in Part 2.

2. Alphabetical list of legislation – gives brief outline of the contents, scope and effect of each Act.

3. Recommended reading – gives a list of general reading and of more specific material under appropriate subject headings.

   The publications listed have been selected as the most useful in their particular fields and are available, together with further books and articles on the subject,

---

* NB The author's consultancy, Industrial Relations Workshop, can be contacted for professional advice and assistance with industrial tribunal cases, appeals to EAT, drawing up contracts of employment and handbooks, etc, on 0181–979–1020.

from the IPD library. Information staff will be pleased to help members with any queries.

4. The index – designed to help readers follow particular topics through the various bits of legislation relating to them.

Acknowledgements

The author wishes to thank Marilyn Arnott, IPD Librarian, who prepared the bibliography. The extracts from the IPM Digest/PM Plus are reproduced by kind permission of the Institute.

Dedication

This book is dedicated to the memory of Deirdre Gill, who was IPM Assistant Director, Information and Advisory Services, a friend and mentor.

NB Throughout this publication the male gender has, in general, been used for convenience but it should be read to include the female gender.

Part 1
Chronological List of Legislation

1814	Apprentices Act
1831 to 1940	Truck Acts (repealed)
1870	Apportionment Act
1913	Trade Union Act (repealed/consolidated)
1919	Sex Disqualification (Removal) Act
1920	Employment of Women, Young Persons and Children Act
1933 to 1969	Children and Young Persons Acts
1936	Public Health Act
1938	Young Persons (Employment) Act (repealed)
	Disabled Persons (Employment) Acts 1944 and 1958 (employment provisions repealed)
1944 and 1973	Education Acts
1950 to 1965	Shop Acts
1960	Payment of Wages Act (repealed)
1961	Factories Act
1963	Offices, Shops and Railway Premises Act
1964	Industrial Training Act
	Trade Union (Amalgamations) Act (repealed/consolidated)
	Young Persons (Employment Act) (repealed)
1969	Employers' Liability (Defective Equipment) Act
	Employers' Liability (Compulsory Insurance) Act
	Family Law Reform Act
1970	Equal Pay Act
1971	Attachment of Earnings Act
	Banking and Financial Dealings Act
	Fire Precautions Act
	Immigration Act
1972	Children Act
	Employment Medical Advisory Services Act
	European Communities Act – Treaty of Rome
1973	Education (Work Experience) Act
	Employment Agencies Act
	Employment of Children Act
	Employment and Training Act
1974	Health and Safety at Work etc. Act
	Rehabilitation of Offenders Act
	Trade Union and Labour Relations Act (repealed/consolidated)
1975	Employment Protection Act (repealed/consolidated)
	Industry Act
	Sex Discrimination Act
	Social Security Act (repealed/consolidated)

	Social Security Pensions Act
1976	Race Relations Act
	Trade Union and Labour Relations (Amendment) Act (repealed/consolidated)
1977	Job Release Act
	Patents Act
	Unfair Contract Terms Act
	Safety Representatives and Safety Committees Regulations 1977 (SI 1977 No. 500)
1978	Employment Protection (Consolidation) Act (repealed/consolidated)
	Employment (Continental Shelf) Act
	Employment Subsidies Act
1979	Wages Council Act (repealed)
1980	Employment Act (repealed/consolidated)
	Social Security (No. 2) Act (repealed/consolidated)
	Industry Act
	Reserve Forces Act
1981	Industry Act
	Employment and Training Act
	Transfer of Undertakings (Protection of Employment) Regulations
1982	Industrial Training Act
	Agricultural Training Board Act
	Employment Act (repealed/consolidated)
	Oil and Gas (Enterprise) Act
	Social Security and Housing Benefits Act (largely repealed/consolidated)
	Social Security (Medical Evidence, Claims and Payments) Amendment Regulations
1983	Equal Pay (Amendment) Regulations
1984	Data Protection Act
	Health and Social Security Act (largely repealed/consolidated)
	Trade Union Act (repealed/consolidated)
1985	Companies Act
	Insolvency Act
	Reserve Forces (Safeguard of Employment) Act
	Social Security Act (largely repealed/consolidated)
1986	Insolvency Act
	Sex Discrimination Act
	Social Security Act (repealed/consolidated)
	Wages Act (repealed/consolidated)
1987	Fire Safety and Safety of Places of Sport Act
1988	Access to Medical Reports Act

Copyright, Designs and Patents Act
Employment Act (repealed/consolidated)
Income and Corporation Taxes Act
Local Government Act
Social Security Act (repealed/consolidated)
1989 Dock Work Act
Employment Act
Finance Act
Local Government and Housing Act
Social Security Act
1990 Access to Health Records Act
Computer Misuse Act
Employment Act (repealed/consolidated)
Finance Act
Food Safety Act
Social Security Act (repealed/consolidated)
1991 Finance Act
Statutory Sick Pay Act (repealed/consolidated)
1992 Further and Higher Education Act
Social Security Administration Act
Social Security (Consequential Provisions) Act
Social Security Contributions and Benefits Act
Trade Union and Labour Relations (Consolidation) Act 1992

'Six-pack' Health and Safety Regulations:
Health and Safety (Display Screen Equipment) Regulations SI
     1992/2792
Management of Health and Safety at Work Regulations SI
     1992/2051
Manual Handling Operations Regulations SI 1992/2793
Personal Protective Equipment at Work Regulations SI
     1992/2966
Provision and Use of Work Equipment Regulations SI
     1992/2932
Workplace (Health, Safety and Welfare) Regulations SI
     1992/3004

1993 Education Act
Criminal Justice Act
Pension Schemes Act
Sex Discrimination and Equal Pay (Remedies) Regulations SI
     1993 No. 2798
Trade Union Reform and Employment Rights Act
1994 Deregulation and Contracting Out Act
Industrial Tribunals Extension of Jurisdiction (England and

Wales) Order 1994 (SI 1994/1623)/(Scotland – SI
1994/1624)
Race Relations (Remedies) Act
Social Security (Incapacity for Work) Act
Statutory Sick Pay Act
Sunday Trading Act (repealed/consolidated)

1995   Collective Redundancies and Transfer of Undertakings
(Protection of Employment) (Amendment) Regulations SI
1995/2587
Disability Discrimination Act
Job Seekers Act
Pensions Act

1996   Asylum and Immigration Act
Employment Rights Act
Industrial Tribunals Rules of Procedure (Amendment) Rules
1996 (SI 1996 No. 1757)
Industrial Tribunals Act
Reserve Forces Act
Health and Safety (Consultation with Employees) Regulations
1996 (SI 1996 No. 1513)

1997   Police Act

List of abbreviations

EPCA	Employment Protection (Consolidation) Act 1992
ERA	Employment Rights Act 1996
TULRA	Trade Union and Labour Relations (Consolidation) Act 1992
TURER	Trade Union Reform and Employment Rights Act 1993

Part 2
Alphabetical List of Legislation

1 Access to Health Records Act 1990
This Act came into force on 1 November 1991.

1.1 What records are covered?
The Act provides for individuals to have access to any records about their health which have been made by, or on behalf of, a health professional in connection with the 'care' of that individual.

The type of records covered by the Act includes records made by a doctor or by a registered nurse (or by someone acting on their behalf).

'Care' for the purposes of this Act includes *any examination of a patient without requiring that that examination be for purposes of medical treatment* (cf. the more restrictive definition of 'care' in the Access to Medical Reports Act 1988 – *see 2.1 below*).

This means that health records made by occupational health staff may now be the subject of scrutiny by the employee to whom they relate.

1.2 Enforcing the right
(a) *Who may apply?*
An applicant who is the patient, or a person authorised in writing to act on the patient's behalf, may apply to the record holder for access to the record. The applicant has the right to inspect the record or to be given a copy (if the record holder prefers). The applicant is also entitled to a 'translation' where the record is not intelligible without explanation. (It is not clear whether this provision is designed to include a requirement to provide a translation of a doctor's illegible handwriting.)
(b) *Time for compliance*
The time within which a record must be supplied depends on how old the material contained in it is. If all the information in the record is more than 40 days old then the record holder has 40 days to provide the record. Otherwise it must be provided within 21 days of the date of the application.
(c) *Cost*
The cost to the applicant is also dependent on the age of the record. If any of the material in the record is less than 40 days old then no charge may be made for granting access. If the record holder chooses to send the applicant a photocopy, rather than granting access, then he can charge for the cost of photocopying and posting the photocopy to the applicant. Where the whole of the record is more than 40 days old a charge can be made up to the same maximum level as can be charged by a data holder for providing disclosure of data held by him (*see Data Protection Act 1984 – 16.5(c) below*). Here again a charge for photocopying and postage may also be made where a photocopy is given.

1.3 Excluding access

Access may be excluded to any part of a health record:
- which contains information the disclosure of which is likely to cause serious harm to the health of any individual; or
- if disclosure of that part of the record would involve disclosing information about another person who is identifiable from the record; or
- which was made before 1 November 1991.

1.4 Correction of inaccuracies

If a person considers that a health record to which he has been given access is inaccurate, he can ask the record holder to correct it. The record holder may correct the information or, if he does not consider it inaccurate, he can put a note on the relevant part of the record stating that the applicant considers that part of the record to be inaccurate.

In either case the record holder must send a copy of the amended record to the applicant free of charge.

1.5 Void contract terms

To ensure that this Act is not used as a means for people other than the patient (for example, employers!) to get hold of the patient's health record, any contractual term which requires an applicant to give a copy of a health record obtained under this Act to another person is declared void.

2 Access to Medical Reports Act 1988

This Act came into force on 1 January 1989. It relates to medical reports obtained for the purposes of employment (or of insurance).

2.1 Definitions

The Act defines a *medical report* as a report
- relating to the physical or mental health of the individual; which
- is prepared by a medical practitioner who is or who has been responsible for the *clinical care* of the individual; and

care is defined by the Act as including *examination, investigation or diagnosis* **for the purposes of** *or in connection with* **any form of medical treatment.**

Where a one-off medical report is sought from a specialist or from a company doctor who has not been involved in the clinical care of the employee the Act will not apply.

2.2 Notification to employee

Section 3 of the Act provides that no employer/prospective employer may ask a medical practitioner for a medical report, covered by the Act, in respect of an employee unless the individual is notified that the employer proposes to make the application and the individual has notified the employer that he consents to the application being made.

The notification given by an employer must inform the employee of the various rights provided for by the Act, ie:

(a) *The employee's right to withhold his consent to the making of such an application*
   The employee can withhold his consent to any application being made by an employer for such a medical report.

(b) *The employee's right to be given access to the medical practitioner's report before it is supplied to the employer*
   If the employee consents to the report being made and asks that he be given access to it, under this provision, then the medical practitioner must be informed by the employer of the employee's wish to have access to the report before it is given to the employer.

   Under the terms of the Act, however, it appears to be for the employee to make his own arrangements with the medical practitioner to obtain access to the report.

   Whether or not the employee asks for and obtains inspection of the report is significant, since a number of the rights in relation to the report depend upon his having had access to the report.

   If the employee asks for access to the report then the medical practitioner may not pass on the report to the employer unless the employee has either been given access to it (and certain other requirements have been met – *see below*) or 21 days have passed and he has not made arrangements to obtain access to the report.

(c) *The employee's right to notify the medical practitioner directly that he wishes to have access to the report*
   If the individual employee consents to the report being applied for, but does not say that he wants to have access to it before it is passed to his employer, he is allowed to ask the medical practitioner directly to give him access to the report. In such cases, again, the medical practitioner may not pass on the report to the employer unless the employee has either been given access to it (and certain other requirements have been met – *see below*) or 21 days have passed and the employee has not made arrangements to obtain access to the report.

(d) *The employee's right to be given access by a medical practitioner to any medical reports relating to him and supplied by the medical practitioner, for employment purposes, within the previous six months*
   If the employee has consented to any report being applied for, he may ask the medical practitioner to give him access to any such report which he has supplied in the previous six months. (This only applies to Reports made after the Act came into force on 1 January 1989.)

(e) *The employee's right to refuse his consent to the report being given to his employer*
   If the employee has had access to the report then the report can only be passed on to his employer if he consents to this being done.

Once the employee has consented to the report being sought then the individual generally only has further rights under the Act if he has had access to the report. There are two exceptions to this limitation:

- the employee retains the right to access a report made within the previous six months; or
- where the report is one to which he has not been allowed access, despite asking for it, because the medical practitioner has refused access on specified grounds (*see below*). If the whole of the report is covered by these grounds, so that the employee is not entitled to access to any of it, the report may still only be passed on to his employer with his express consent.

(f) *The employee's right to request the medical practitioner, in writing, before giving his consent to the report being supplied, to amend any part of the report which the individual considers to be misleading or incorrect*

The employee may ask the medical practitioner to amend any part/s of a report to which he has had access which he considers to be incorrect or misleading. The medical practitioner may amend the report to the extent that he is prepared so to do. If he is not prepared to amend it, or if he is not prepared to amend it as extensively as the individual might wish, then the individual may ask that a statement of his views be attached to the report. Any such request must also be made in writing.

2.3   Grounds on which a medical practitioner may refuse an individual access to a medical report

A medical practitioner may refuse an individual access to all or parts of a medical report where he considers that disclosure of the report, or of those parts:

- would be likely to 'cause serious harm to the physical or mental health of the individual or others'; or
- would indicate the intentions of the medical practitioner in relation to that individual; or
- would be likely to reveal information about another person without that person's consent; or
- would be likely to reveal the identity of another person (ie a non-health professional) who has given information to the practitioner about the individual – again, unless that person consents to the disclosure.

In any such case the medical practitioner must inform the individual that he considers that the above criteria apply either to all or to parts of the report. In such cases the individual is only entitled to have access to any parts of the report which are not covered by the above prohibitions on disclosure. If the whole of the report is covered by these prohibitions, then the employee is not entitled to access to any of it. However, any such report may only be passed on to his employer, assuming that the employee originally asked for access to it, with the employee's express consent.

2.4   Enforcement of the Act

Enforcement of the Act is through the county court (sheriff's court in Scotland). The Act simply provides that if it appears to the court that any person has failed or is likely to fail to comply with any part of the Act then the court may order that they do comply. Any failure to comply with such an order would, of course, amount to contempt of court.

3   Agricultural Training Board Act 1982

Amended by Employment Act 1989.

Repeals most of the Training Act 1964 as it applied to the Agricultural Training Board and part of Employment and Training Act 1973.

Consolidates the law relating to the Agricultural Training Board.

4   Apportionment Act 1870

The effect of ss 2 and 5 is that 'salaries . . . shall be considered as accruing from day to day, and shall be apportioned in respect of time accordingly'. It is undecided whether or not 'wages' accrue on a daily basis.

5   Apprentices Act 1814

The effect of this Act is that a contract of apprenticeship must be written. If it is not, it will take effect as a contract of employment.

NB A contract of apprenticeship is defined as being a contract of employment for employment protection purposes (*see s 230 Employment Rights Act 1996*).

6   Attachment of Earnings Act 1971

Empowers a court to order that a judgment debt be paid directly by the employer, from the employee's earnings, to the court.

7   Asylum and Immigration Act 1996

Amends the Immigration Act 1971.

For employment purposes, the most important effect of this Act is that it makes it an offence for an employer to employ someone who is not entitled to be in and to work in the UK.

7.1   The offence

(a) An employer commits an offence if:
   (i)   he employs a person of 16 or over (the 'employee')
   (ii) the employee is subject to immigration control; and
      • the employee does not have current valid leave to be in the UK; or
      • the employee's leave is subject to a condition which stops him from taking up that employment. (NB: The reference to 'that employment' is important since an employee who has a work permit, for example, will

be entitled to work in the employment to which the permit relates, but not in any other job.)

(b) In certain cases, even where the employee, *prima facie*, is not entitled to be in, or to work in, the UK an employer may nonetheless employ him. The three situations in which this is permissible were introduced by the Immigration (Restrictions on Employment) Order 1996 SI 1996 No. 3225

   (i)   where an employee, having made a claim for asylum which is still under consideration, has been given written permission to work by the Home Office

   (ii)   where the employee has an appeal pending under Part II of the Immigration Act 1971 – provided that before the appeal was made the employee was entitled to work in the UK

   (iii) if the employee is entitled to work under the Immigration Rules.

7.2   The defence

An employer will have a defence to a potential prosecution for employing someone who is not entitled to be or to work in the UK if before that person's employment began:

(a) the employer was shown a document which appeared to relate to the employee in question (ie it appeared to be both a genuine document and to relate to the employee)

(b) the document was of a description specified by the Secretary of State as being appropriate for these purposes (*see 7.3 below*)

(c) the employer either kept the document itself or a copy of it. (A copy can be either a paper copy or a copy kept on a WORM CD, ie a Write Once Read Many times CD. This means that the CD can only be written on once so that a true, unalterable copy is kept); and

(d) the employer did not know that employing the employee would be unlawful under these provisions.

7.3   Acceptable documents

The Home Office has issued a guide to employers dealing with the requirements under these provisions. A full list of the types of document which are acceptable for purposes of the defence in 7.2 above is contained in the guide which has been sent to all employers. The main documents are as follows:

(a) Usually employers will be provided by new employees with a 'documented National Insurance number' (an official document on which the person's National Insurance number is stated). This could be:

   • A document issued by a previous employer, such as a P45, a pay slip or a P60

   • A document issued by the Inland Revenue, the Benefits Agency, the Contributions Agency or the Employment Service (or their Northern Ireland equivalents) such as a NINO card (the newer plastic cards or the older-style cards) or a letter issued by one of the government bodies mentioned above.

It should be noted that documents showing a National Insurance number with a 'TN' prefix is a temporary National Insurance number and is not acceptable.

(b) a passport showing that the person is a British or EU citizen or which has a stamp on it showing that the person has a right be or to remain in the UK

(c) naturalisation papers

(d) a work permit or a letter from the immigration authorities saying that the person has a right to work in the UK.

7.4 Race discrimination

It is obviously important that all job applicants are treated the same so that there are no accusations or feelings that people are being discriminated against on grounds of their race. One way of dealing with this is to ask for the same documents from all those who are going to be offered a job. Employers may have their own list of documents which all employees are required to produce. These might include, for example, a P45, P60, other documented NI number, passport, etc.

7.5 Further information

(a) There is a helpline which is available to anyone with a query on these requirements – 0181–649–7878. The Employer's Guide is also available on the Internet at http://www.open.gov.uk/home_off/ind.htm

(b) The CRE has issued provisional guidance on good practice for employers in dealing with these requirements.

8 Banking and Financial Dealings Act 1971

Amended by Employment Act 1989.

Repeals previous legislation relating to bank holidays and substitutes a schedule of bank holidays.

9 Children and Young Persons Acts 1933–1969, Children Act 1972, Employment of Women, Young Persons and Children Act 1920

Amended by Employment Act 1989. The 1933 Act is amended by Manual Handling Operations Regulations 1992 SI 1992/2793.

These Acts restrict the employment of children. They are repealed by the Employment Act 1989 insofar as they restricted the employment of women and young persons.

10 Collective Redundancies and Transfer of Undertakings (Protection of Employment) (Amendment) Regulations SI 1995/2587

Amend the Employment Protection (Consolidation) Act 1978 (now consolidated into ERA), TULRA and Transfer of Undertakings (Protection of Employment) Regulations 1981.

These regulations provide for representation by employee representatives as an alternative to trade union representation in relation to:

(a) consultation about proposed redundancies (see also 102.10); and

(b) consultation about transfers of undertakings (see also 105.1).

11   Companies Acts 1985 and 1989

11A   Companies Act 1985

The Companies Act 1985 is a consolidation of the previous Companies Acts. The Companies Act 1985 is of great importance to the employment, duties and liabilities of company directors.

Matters of particular concern in the personnel field:

11A.1 The Act obliges companies to keep a copy or memorandum of their directors' contracts of employment for inspection by members of the company (ie shareholders)

11A.2 A contract of employment with a director, which is to be for more than five years and which includes any restriction on the company's ability to terminate the contract by notice, may only be made if approved by a general meeting of the company following due notification of the terms of the agreement.

11A.3 The Act puts directors under a duty to perform their functions so as to promote the interests of the company's employees as well as its shareholders. It also includes within the powers of a company, where this is not specified, a power for the company to make adequate provision for its employees (or those of a subsidiary company) where the company is winding up or being transferred.

11A.4 The Act requires certain matters to be disclosed in directors' reports where the average number of employees in a company in each week of the relevant financial year is more than 250. These are:

(a) the policy which has been applied in relation to disabled employees during that year:

- for giving full and fair consideration to applications for employment by disabled people
- for continuing the employment of and retraining of those who become disabled whilst in the company's employment
- for training, career development and promotion of disabled employees generally within the company.

(b) the action taken during that year to introduce, maintain or develop arrangements aimed at:

- systematically providing employees with information on matters of concern to them as employees
- consulting employees/their representatives on a regular basis so that employees' views can be taken into account in making decisions that are likely to affect employees' interests

- encouraging employee involvement in the company's performance through employee share schemes or by other means
- achieving a common awareness on the part of all employees of the financial and economic factors affecting the performance of the company.

11B   Companies Act 1989

Amends the Companies Act 1985 to require that all elements of remuneration paid to directors and any payments for loss of office be disclosed. This applies whether the payments are made by the company itself or by a holding or subsidiary company.

12   Company Securities (Insider Dealing) Act 1985

Repealed and replaced by Part V Criminal Justice Act 1993 (*see below, section 15*).

13   Computer Misuse Act 1990

Makes it a criminal offence for a person knowingly to try to gain unauthorised access to a computer program or to any data held on a computer. The Act also makes it an offence to try to modify any of the contents of a computer without authority.

14   Copyright, Designs and Patents Act 1988

Repeals the Copyright Act 1956 and consolidates the law of copyright.
14.1 Determines the ownership of the copyright of literary, dramatic or other artistic works and provides that the copyright in such a work created by an employee in the course of his employment belongs to the employer, subject to any agreement to the contrary.
14.2 The copyright in anything done outside the course of the employee's duties belongs to the employee.
14.3 The ownership of a copyright may be determined by contract.
14.4 Computer software is subject to copyright.

15   Criminal Justice Act 1993

Part V repeals and replaces the Company Securities (Insider Dealing) Act 1985.
15.1 Prohibits any individual from knowingly dealing in securities of any company when he has information 'as an insider'. It also prohibits him from encouraging anyone else to deal in such securities or disclosing the information which he has 'as an insider' to anyone else; other than in the proper performance of his employment or profession.
15.2 'Inside information' is information which:
- relates to particular securities
- is specific

- is unpublished
- would be likely, if published, to have a significant effect on the price of any securities.

15.3 A person has information 'as an insider', *inter alia*, if
- it is inside information; and
- he has obtained it through his employment; or
- he has obtained it from someone who obtained it through his (the other person's) employment.

16   Data Protection Act 1984

Provides for the compulsory registration of users of personal data and for individual access to personal data concerning the individual. The Act also provides for compensation for misuse of personal data and for compensation to data subjects for inaccuracies. The main framework of the Act is as follows:

16.1   Definitions

Data is information which is recorded in a form in which it can be processed automatically. *Processing* for these purposes means augmenting, updating, amending, deleting or extracting information. This definition excludes manual systems.

Personal data is data which relates to a living individual who is identifiable either from the data alone or with the aid of any other information in the data user's possession. Personal data includes any expression of opinion about the individual, but not any expression of intention the data user may have in respect of him.

Data subject is an individual who is the subject of personal data.

16.2   Data protection principles

The Act lays down eight data protection principles and, unusually, it also provides interpretation for the application of those principles. The principles are these:

(a) The information contained in personal data must be obtained, and the personal data processed, fairly and lawfully.

   In deciding whether data was obtained fairly and lawfully, the purpose for which it was obtained and used, and questions as to whether any person who provided the information was deceived or misled as to that purpose, must be taken into account.

(b) Personal data is only to be held for one or more specified and lawful purposes.

(c) Personal data is not to be used or disclosed in a manner incompatible with the specified purpose/s.

(d) Personal data must be adequate, relevant and not excessive in relation to the purposes for which it is held.

(e) Personal data must be accurate and updated if necessary.

(f) Personal data must not be kept for longer than is necessary to fulfil the purpose for which it is held (this principle is subject to an exception where data is used for historical, statistical or research purposes. In such cases, provided the data subject is not likely to suffer any damage or distress thereby, the data may be kept indefinitely).

(g) The data subject is entitled, at reasonable intervals and without undue delay:
- to be informed whether he is the subject of personal data held by a data user; and
- to have access to such data and to have the data corrected or erased where appropriate.

16.3 Registration of data users and computer bureaux

The Act provides for the establishment of a Data Protection Registrar. All data users and computer bureaux (with few exceptions) must register with the Registrar, and must furnish him with:
- the name and address of the data user
- a description of the data held by him, the purposes for which it is held or used, the sources from which he obtains the data, and a description of any persons to whom he intends or may wish to disclose the data
- a description of any countries or territories outside the UK to which he intends or may wish directly or indirectly to transfer the data (ie to help enforce the data protection legislation which restricts personal data from being sent to countries outside the EU where there is no similar protection)
- one or more addresses for receipt of requests for subject-access to the data.

16.4 Supervision

The Registrar has some powers to refuse applications for registration and orders may be made preventing data from being taken out of the UK. Enforcement notices may also be issued where any person appears to be in breach of the data protection principles.

A Data Protection Tribunal is established to hear appeals from any refusal by the Registrar of an application for registration or alteration of registered particulars and from any order made by the Registrar.

16.5 Individual rights

An individual is entitled to be informed, on request, whether or not the data user holds personal data about him and if so to receive a copy of that data, in intelligible form, within 40 days of his request. *But:*

(a) the data user is entitled to refuse to comply with any such request until he obtains reasonable proof of the identity of the person making the request

(b) the data user need not comply if the data also relates to another identifiable individual unless the data user is satisfied that the other individual has given his consent to disclosure

(c) the data user may also require a fee from the data subject for disclosure. This fee is subject to a prescribed maximum.

16.6   Exemptions

Total exemption from the provisions of the Act:
(a) data held for purposes of safeguarding national security
(b) payroll, pensions and accounting data: such data may not be used for any other purpose, nor may it be disclosed except for certain lawful purposes – ie for audit purposes and for purposes of giving information about the data subject's financial affairs. Payroll and pensions data may also be disclosed to the person responsible for making payments, for purposes of actuarial advice or for giving information relevant to the health or injury of a data subject. Apart from these exceptions disclosure may only be made with the consent of the data subject.
(c) data held by unincorporated clubs regarding their members
(d) names and addresses held for mailing or distribution lists (provided the data subject has not objected to inclusion on that list)
(e) data which is required by law to be publicly available
(f) data held for purposes of text preparation only (eg on word processors)
(g) data held by an individual for domestic or recreational purposes.

There are further exemptions from the general right of data subjects to have access to personal data concerning them. The Home Secretary may by order exempt other types of information, including information regarding the physical or mental health of a data subject.

17   Deregulation and Contracting Out Act 1994

Amends the Employment Agencies Act 1973, Betting Gaming and Lotteries Act 1963 and Shops Act 1950.
    Is in part repealed by and consolidated into the Employment Rights Act 1996.

17.1   Employment agencies

(a) Removes the requirement for employment agencies and employment businesses to be licensed
(b) Prohibition Orders
    (i)   The Act introduces a system through which an industrial tribunal can, on the application of the Secretary of State, make an order either:
        • prohibiting an individual from being involved in an employment agency or business; or
        • imposing conditions on their involvement.
    (ii) Before making any such order the tribunal must be satisfied that the individual was responsible, or partly responsible, for the improper conduct of the business. Where there is more than one person who manages the business all are equally responsible for any misconduct of the business unless they can show that it happened without their connivance or consent and without negligence on their part.
    (iii) A prohibition or condition imposed by an industrial tribunal can last for a period of up to 10 years.

(iv) A person on whom an order is made can apply to have the order varied or can appeal to the EAT against the tribunal's decision (on a point of law only).

(v) Failure to comply with a Prohibition Order is dealt with by criminal law sanctions.

17.2 Sunday working

Betting shop workers were given similar rights to those given to other shop workers under the Sunday Trading Act 1994 (the provisions for both betting shop and other shop workers are now consolidated into the Employment Rights Act 1996 qv). (See 36.5.)

Ss 17 and 22 of the Shops Act 1950 are both repealed. These sections

* gave shop workers time off in lieu for Sunday working; and
* restricted shop workers from having to work more than three Sundays in any month.

18 Disabled Persons (Employment) Acts 1944 and 1958

Are largely repealed and replaced, for employment purposes, by the Disability Discrimination Act 1995 (qv).

19 Disability Discrimination Act 1995

Repeals much of the Disabled Persons (Employment) Act 1944 and amends Disabled Persons (Employment) Act 1958, Chronically Sick and Disabled Persons Act 1970, Employment Protection (Consolidation) Act 1978, Local Government and Housing Act 1989, Education Act 1993.

19.1 Disability

A person who has a physical or mental impairment which has a long-term and substantial adverse effect on his ability to carry out normal day-to-day activities has a disability for purposes of the Act. It should be remembered that the rights under the Act affect people with disabilities individually so that if a person with one leg is discriminated against by being refused a job because of his disability, it is no defence for an employer to have hired a person with one arm to do that job.

1 'Impairment'
   (a) There is no general definition of what an impairment is.
   (b) A mental impairment only amounts to a disability if it results from an illness which is clinically well recognised.
   (c) Specific conditions may be declared by regulations to be or not to be impairments for purposes of the Act. The Disability Discrimination (Meaning of Disability) Regulations 1996 (SI 1996/1455) specify certain matters as not being impairments:
      * addictions – unless they originally arose from medically prescribed drugs

- tendencies to setting fires, stealing, physical or sexual abuse, exhibitionism or voyeurism
- hay fever – although this can be taken into account where its effects aggravate another impairment
- tattoos and body piercing which have been done for non-medical purposes.

2   'Substantial adverse effect'
  (a) There is no definition of what amounts to a 'substantial adverse effect'.
  (b) Regulations can prescribe that a particular kind of effect on the ability of a person to perform normal day-to-day activities shall or shall not be considered to be 'substantial'.
  (c) Severe disfigurement
      (i)   An impairment which consists of severe disfigurement is to be treated as having a long-term substantial adverse effect on a person's ability to carry out normal day-to-day activities.
      (ii)   Cases where severe disfigurement is not to be treated as having that effect may be prescribed by Regulations. Tattoos and voluntary body piercing have already been proscribed for these purposes (*see Disability Discrimination (Meaning of Disability) Regulations 1996 (SI 1996/1455)*).
  (d) Impact of medical treatment
      Where an impairment would be likely to have a substantial adverse effect on a person but for the fact that measures are being taken to correct or to treat it, the impairment is nonetheless treated as having a substantial adverse effect.
      (i)   'Measures' include medical treatment and the use of prostheses or other aids.
      (ii)   This does not apply to people whose eyesight is correctable by glasses or contact lenses.
      (iii)   Regulations can be made to exclude other cases where a person receiving treatment or subject to other measures is not to be considered as substantially adversely affected by the impairment in question.

3   Long-term effect
  (a) An impairment is considered to have a long-term effect if:
      (i)   it has lasted 12 months or more
      (ii)   it is likely to last for at least 12 months; or
      (iii)   it is likely to last for the rest of that person's life.
  (b) Guidance may be issued by the Secretary of State (which must be taken into account by any court or tribunal, where it is relevant) as to whether any impairment may or may not be considered as having a long-term effect.
  (c) Recurrence

(i)   If the condition ceases to have a substantial adverse effect on the person's ability to carry out normal day-to-day activities but the effect is expected to recur then it is to be treated as continuing to have that effect.

(ii)   Regulations can prescribe:
  • when the threat of recurrence is to be ignored for these purposes; and
  • circumstances where an effect which would not otherwise be considered long term is to be considered to be long term and vice versa.

4   Normal day-to-day activities
  (a) The impairment must affect one or more of the following if it is to affect 'normal day-to-day activities':
    (i)   mobility
    (ii)   manual dexterity
    (iii) physical co-ordination
    (iv)   continence
    (v)   ability to lift, carry or otherwise move day-to-day objects
    (vi)   speech, hearing or eyesight
    (vii) memory or ability to concentrate, learn or understand; or
    (viii) perception of the risk of physical danger.
  (b) Regulations may prescribe where an impairment does or does not have any of the above effects or where it is to be taken as not affecting the person's ability to carry out normal day-to-day activities.

5   Deemed disability
  (a) Registered disabled: A person who was registered as disabled on 12 January 1995 is to be taken to be disabled for three years from that date and is thereafter treated as having been disabled during that period. Under the new provisions disabled people are no longer registered as such.
  (b) Progressive conditions: A person who is suffering from a progressive condition which is likely to result in his having a substantial impairment is to be treated as having a substantial impairment (examples of such conditions include cancer, MS, muscular dystrophy, and HIV infection).
  (c) Past disabilities: The Act applies to those with past disabilities, and, with some modifications, applies to those who are currently disabled.

19.2 Small employers

None of the duties under the Act apply to employers with fewer than 20 employees. The maximum number of employees an employer may have whilst being considered a 'small employer' under the Act, may be reduced by the Secretary of State by Order.

19.3 Discrimination by employers

1 It is unlawful for an employer to discriminate against a disabled person (in relation to employment at an establishment in Great Britain):

(a) at the pre-employment stage:
   (i)   in the arrangements he makes for determining who should be offered that employment
   (ii) in the terms on which he offers that employment
   (iii) by refusing to offer, or deliberately not offering him, that employment; and

(b) against a disabled employee of his:
   (i)   in the terms of employment which he offers
   (ii) in the opportunities which he affords him for
      • promotion
      • transfer
      • training; or
      • receiving any other benefit.
         • 'Benefits' include facilities or services.
         • This does not apply where the employer is concerned with the provision of benefits of that description to the public (whether or not for payment) or to a section of the public which includes the employee unless:
            – what is provided to the public is materially different from what is provided to his employees; or
            – the provision of the benefit in question is regulated by the employee's contract of employment; or
            – the benefits relate to training (s 4(3)).
   (iii) by refusing/failing to afford him any of the above opportunities

(c) by dismissing the employee or subjecting him to any other detriment.

2 'Employment'
As with the sex and race discrimination legislation, 'employment' is widely defined. It means employment under a contract of apprenticeship or employment or under a contract personally to do any work. As such, it includes those who are self-employed and who are working through employment agencies provided they are hired to do the work personally.

3 'Discrimination'

(a) An employer discriminates against a disabled person if for a reason related to that disability (NB this is concerned with the individual's particular disability, not with the fact that the person is disabled in general terms):

   • he treats him less favourably than he treats or would treat others to whom that reason does not or would not apply; and
   • he cannot show that the treatment in question is justified.

(i) 'Justification'
- Treatment is only 'justified' if the reason for it:
  - is material to the circumstances of the particular case; and
  - substantial.
- Regulations can be made to provide when any treatment is and is not to be taken to be justified. Such regulations may make provision:
  - by reference to the cost of providing any benefit; and
  - in relation to benefits under an occupational pension scheme with a view to enabling uniform rates of contributions to be maintained (*see Disability Discrimination (Employment) Regulations 1996 (SI 1996 No. 1456)*).
- Where an employer has failed to comply with the duty to make reasonable adjustments to accommodate a disabled person (*see 19.4 below*), then any question of whether or not the employer was justified in any discrimination against that person has to be approached as if the employer had made any reasonable adjustments which were necessary. Or, put another way, the employer cannot rely on his failure to make reasonable adjustments as justification for discriminating on grounds of disability.

(ii) NB Apart from the requirement to make reasonable adjustments (*see 19.4 below*), the Act, insofar as it deals with discrimination in the employment field, does not require an employer to give a disabled person better treatment than he would give to any other person.

(b) An employer also discriminates against a disabled person if:
  (i) he fails to comply with any duty to make reasonable adjustments (*see 19.4*); and
  (ii) he cannot show that his failure to comply with the duty in question is justified (*for 'justification', see 19.3.3(a) above*).

19.4 Employer's duty to make adjustments

1 The duty to make adjustments is enshrined in s 6 of the Act:
  (a) Where
    (i) arrangements made by or on behalf of an employer; or
    (ii) any physical feature of premises occupied by the employer
    place the disabled person concerned at a substantial disadvantage by comparison to people who are not disabled, the employer is under a duty to take such steps as it is reasonable for him to take in all the circumstances of the case, to prevent the arrangements or feature from having that effect.

(b) Regulations can be made
   (i) to say what are and are not physical features for these purposes (*see Reg. 9 Disability Discrimination (Employment) Regulations 1996 (SI 1996 No. 1456)*)
   (ii) to say when certain arrangements or physical features are and are not to be taken to cause substantial disadvantage to disabled people; and
   (iii) to add to the duties imposed by s 6.
2 General limitations on the duty under s 6:
   (a) The duty to make adjustments under s 6 does not apply to:
       (i) any benefit under an occupational pension scheme; or
       (ii) any benefit payable in money or monies worth under a scheme or arrangement for the benefit of employees in respect of:
           ● termination of service
           ● retirement, old age or death
           ● accident, injury, sickness or invalidity
           ● any other prescribed matter (*see the Disability Discrimination (Employment) Regulations 1996 (SI 1996 No. 1456)*).
   (b) The duty only applies for purposes of determining whether or not an employer has discriminated against a disabled person and a breach of this duty is not therefore actionable otherwise than within the terms of the DDA.
3 'The disabled person concerned' for purposes of s 6 is:
   (a) in the case of discriminatory arrangements for determining to whom employment should be offered any disabled person who:
       (i) is a job applicant; or
       (ii) who has notified the employer that he might be an applicant for the job; or
   (b) in any other case a person who is:
       (i) an applicant for the job; or
       (ii) an employee.
4 Reasonable steps:
   (a) The requirement for an employer to take reasonable steps to prevent any *arrangements* he has made (as opposed to physical features) from having the effect of placing a disabled person at a substantial disadvantage does not apply to:
       (i) dismissal
       (ii) or subjecting the person to any other detriment.

At first glance this might seem to mean that an employer is under no duty, for example, to change a redundancy policy which has the effect of selecting disabled people for redundancy before able-bodied people. Any such discrimination would, however, be subject to the general requirement not to discriminate against the disabled person in question by dismissing him or subjecting him to a detriment. (A detriment might occur in this type of case if, for example, the employee was moved to another, less desirable job, rather than being dismissed in the redundancy situation.)

(b) The type of steps which it may be reasonable for an employer to take to obviate the adverse impact of any discriminatory effect are exemplified by the Act itself. These include:

(i)   making adjustments to premises

(ii)   allocating some of the disabled person's duties to another person

(iii)   transferring the disabled person to fill an existing vacancy

(iv)   altering his hours of work

(v)   assigning him to a different place of work

(vi)   allowing him to be absent during working hours for rehabilitation, assessment or treatment

(vii)   giving him or arranging for him to be given training

(viii) acquiring or modifying equipment for that person's use

(ix)   modifying instructions or reference manuals

(x)   modifying procedures for testing or assessment of the disabled person

(xi)   providing a reader or interpreter

(xii)   providing supervision.

However, these are only examples and the steps which it may be reasonable for an employer to take will depend on the circumstances. For example, in the case of a job applicant it would normally be reasonable to hold the interviews in a place which is accessible to the candidate and at a time which does not prevent him, because of his disability, from attending the interview.

(c) In determining whether it is reasonable for an employer to have to take a particular step in order to prevent a disabled person being put at a substantial disadvantage as compared with a person who is not disabled, the following must be considered:

(i)   the extent to which the step would prevent the effect in question

(ii)   the extent to which it is practicable for the employer to take the step

(iii)   the financial and other costs which would be incurred by the employer in taking the step and the extent to which taking it would disrupt his activities

(iv)   the extent of the employer's financial and other resources

(v)   the availability to the employer of financial or other assistance with respect to taking the step.

(d) Regulations may

(i)   define prescribed steps which it is and is not reasonable to take; and

(ii)   the circumstances in which it is or is not reasonable for an employer to have to take those steps.

(iii)   These regulations may make provisions by reference to the cost of taking any such measures.

5   Limitation on the duty to take steps
An employer has no duty to take steps if the employer did not know and could not reasonably be expected to know, in the case of a disabled applicant or potential applicant for employment, that the person concerned is or may be an applicant for employment.

19.5   Victimisation

1   A person victimises another if he treats that other less favourably because he has:
(a) brought proceedings against any person under the DDA
(b) given evidence or information in connection with any such proceedings
(c) otherwise done anything under the DDA in relation to any person
(d) alleged that anyone has contravened the DDA.
2   A person victimises another if he treats that other less favourably because he believes or suspects that the victim has done or intends to do any of the things set out in 19.5.1.
3   A person cannot claim victimisation if he has made a false allegation in bad faith.

19.6   Enforcement

1   Enforcement in the employment field is through the tribunal system. A case must be brought within three months of the discrimination complained of. As with sex and race discrimination claims, the tribunal can extend time for presenting a complaint if it considers that it is just and equitable to do so in the circumstances of the case.
2   Where a tribunal finds that a complaint is well-founded, it can:
(a) make a declaration as to the applicant's and the employer's rights in relation to the matters complained of
(b) order the employer to pay compensation (the compensation in these cases, as with sex and race discrimination, is without limit and can include damages for injury to feeling caused by the discrimination)
(c) recommend that the employer takes such action as the tribunal considers reasonable to obviate or reduce the adverse effect on the applicant of the matter complained of. The tribunal can also specify the time within which such action must be taken. If the employer fails to take the recommended action then the tribunal can award additional compensation.

DfEE Code of Practice 1996

In 1996 the DfEE produced a Code of Practice for the elimination of discrimination in the field of employment against disabled persons or persons who have had a disability. The Code is not legally binding in its own right, but its provisions are admissible in evidence before a tribunal or a court. The Code as well as going through the law on disabilities and employment, and giving helpful examples of the provisions of the DDA, makes a few fundamental suggestions which employers should take into account:

1. Do not make assumptions – talk to the individual disabled person to see what the effects of their disability might be. In most cases they will have a better idea than you as to what their limitations are and how any limitations can be got round.
2. Consider if expert advice is needed – whilst there is no obligation to get expert advice, it may be helpful to do so, especially where the person is newly disabled and therefore less likely to know what his limitations will be (if any) due to the disability.
3. Plan ahead – where changes are being made in buildings, etc. consider the possible effect on potential disabled job applicants.
4. Promote equal opportunities – employers who have equal opportunities policies are likely, says the Code, to have that counted in their favour by a court or tribunal.

It should be borne in mind, in the context of promoting equal opportunities, that:
  (a) the duty to disabled people is owed to them as individuals rather than as a class; and
  (b) there is no prohibition on positive discrimination in favour of the disabled – provided that there is no discrimination as between people with different disabilities. (NB There are provisions which do allow for discrimination between people with different types of disabilities, but these are limited broadly to charities which are set up to deal with particular types of disability.)

Employers needing specialist help regarding the employment of people with disabilities should contact their local Placing, Assessment and Counselling Team (PACT). PACTs are part of the Employment Service.

20   Dock Work Act 1989

(a) Abolished the Dock Workers Employment Scheme and the National Dock Labour Board.
(b) Makes provisions for redundancy payments for dock workers who are made redundant and provides that those registered as dock workers at the date that the Act was passed are to have their previous service whilst registered counted towards their period of continuous employment.

21   Education Acts 1944 to 1973

Amended by Further and Higher Education Act 1992 and Education Act 1993.
  Define *child* and *young person*.

22   Education Act 1993

Amends Education Act 1944, Factories Act 1961, Education (Work Experience) Act 1973, Sex Discrimination Act 1975, Race Relations Act 1976, Employment Act 1989.

Amended by Disability Discrimination Act 1995.

Defines compulsory school age. Minimum school-leaving age is the end of the school year in which the individual reaches 16 or where he will be 16 before the beginning of the following school year.

23   Education (Work Experience) Act 1973

Amended by Employment Act 1990 and Education Act 1993.

Enables education authorities to arrange for children under school-leaving age to have work experience as part of their education in their last year of compulsory schooling.

24   Employers' Liability (Compulsory Insurance) Act 1969

Amended by Police Act 1997.

Prescribes that all employers must insure against liability for personal injury and disease sustained by their employees and arising out of, or in the course of, their employment in Great Britain.

25   Employers' Liability (Defective Equipment) Act 1969

Amended by Police Act 1997.

Makes an employer liable, without proof of fault on his part, in all cases where an employee sustains personal injury in the course of his employment 'in consequence of a defect in equipment provided by his employer for the purposes of the employer's business'.

26   Employment Acts 1980 to 1988 and 1990

Largely repealed and consolidated by TULRA.

27   Employment Act 1989

Amended by Employment Act 1990, Further and Higher Education Act 1992 and Education Act 1993.

Amends Employment of Women, Young Persons and Children Act 1920, Shops Act 1950, Factories Act 1961, Children and Young Persons Act 1963, Employment and Training Act 1973, Health and Safety at Work, etc. Act 1974, Employment Protection Act 1975, Social Security Act 1975, Sex Discrimination Acts 1975 and 1986, Race Relations Act 1976, Employment Protection (Consolidation) Act 1978, Employment and Training Act 1981, Agricultural Training Board Act 1982, Industrial Training Act 1982, Employment Act 1988. Repeals Young Persons (Employment) Acts 1938 and 1964.

27.1 Sex discrimination law amendments

Unusually for an 'Employment Act', the 1989 Act is primarily concerned with updating the Sex Discrimination Act 1975 to bring it into line with the European Directive on sex discrimination.

(a) *Removing the effects of discriminatory legislation passed before the Sex Discrimination Act 1975*

Where any provision of an Act which was passed before the Sex Discrimination Act 1975 imposes a requirement to do anything which would be discriminatory under the SDA 1975, then that provision is of 'no effect'. This provision extends to cover post-1975 re-enactments of pre-1975 Acts and also includes any statutory instrument made under any such Act – whether the statutory instrument was made before or after the 1975 Act was passed.

The Secretary of State for Employment is also given power to amend, revoke or repeal any such provision of any such Act or of any statutory instrument made under any such Act.

(b) *Circumstances in which discrimination is permissible*

The Act provides that discrimination against women is not unlawful insofar as it is necessary:

(i) to comply with any existing (ie pre-SDA 1975) statutory provision (or any statutory instrument passed under any such statute) concerning the protection of women in relation to pregnancy, maternity, or risks specifically affecting women; or

(ii) to comply with the requirement to take care of the health and safety of women in relation to pregnancy, maternity, or risks specifically affecting women.

(c) *Exemptions from the provisions of the SDA 1975*

(i) Employment as a Head Teacher or Principal of an educational establishment where any instrument relating to the establishment requires that its head be of a particular religious order

(ii) Employment as the Head, a fellow or any other member of the academic staff of any college or similar institution where any instrument relating to the establishment requires that the position in question be filled by a woman.

(d) *Discrimination as regards training*

(i) Section 14 of the Sex Discrimination Act 1975, which was concerned with the provision of training by vocational training bodies, is re-enacted with amendments (the equivalent provision of the Race Relations Act 1976 is similarly amended).

(ii) The Secretary of State is empowered to allow for discrimination in favour of single parents in relation to certain types of training.

27.2   Removal of restrictions on hours of work, etc. in respect of women and young persons

Most of the restrictions on the hours of employment for women and young persons are lifted. This legislation does not, however, affect the restrictions on the employment of 'children' (ie those under minimum school-leaving age).

27.3   Race discrimination

(a) *Discrimination as regards training*
    Section 13 of the Race Relations Act 1976, which was concerned with the provision of training by vocational training bodies, is re-enacted with amendments (the equivalent provision of the Sex Discrimination Act 1975 is similarly amended).

(b) *Safety helmets*
    A Sikh who is wearing a turban is exempted from any legal requirement to wear a safety helmet on a construction site. If he is injured, however, then any liability on the person causing the injury is limited to the damage which would have been done if the employee had been wearing a safety helmet.

28   Employment Agencies Act 1973

Amended by Employment Protection Act 1975, Deregulation and Contracting Out Act 1994, Police Act 1997.

Lays down rules for running employment agencies and employment businesses. The former requirement for employment agencies to be licensed was removed by the Deregulation and Contracting Out Act 1994.

29   Employment and Training Act 1973

Amended by Employment Protection Act 1975, Employment and Training Act 1981, Agricultural Training Board Act 1982, Industrial Training Act 1982 and Employment Acts 1988 and 1989.

The Manpower Services Commission (MSC) is established as an independent body to run the public employment and training services. The two executive arms of the MSC set up by this Act have now been disbanded.

30   Employment (Continental Shelf) Act 1978

Amended by Trade Union and Labour Relations (Consolidation) Act 1992.

The Oil and Gas (Enterprise) Act 1982 contains provisions repealing the following extensions of the sex and race discrimination legislation. An Order will need to be made under the 1982 Act to give effect to these repeals.

The Act extends the rights under the Sex Discrimination Act 1975 and Race Relations Act 1976 to those working on 'cross-boundary' oil fields in the North Sea. A 'cross-boundary' oil field is one which is partly inside and partly outside United Kingdom territorial waters.

31 Employment Medical Advisory Services Act 1972

Amends Factories Act 1961.

Sets up the Employment Medical Advisory Service (EMAS). Allows an EMAS medical adviser to serve notice on a factory occupier requiring the occupier to allow for medical examination of employees in factories where the medical adviser is of the opinion that an employee's health has been, is being or may be injured by reason of the work he is being, or may be, called upon to do. Provides for EMAS medical advisers to take over medical examinations required by the Factories Act 1961. Payment for these services is made to the Secretary of State.

32 Employment of Children Act 1973

Amends Children and Young Persons Act 1933.

Gives local education authorities powers to supervise, prohibit and restrict the employment of children in their areas.

33 Employment of Women, Young Persons and Children Act 1920

Amended by Employment of Women, Young Persons and Children Act 1936 and Employment Act 1989.

Restricts employment of children in industrial undertakings.

34 Employment Protection Act 1975 (EPA) (repealed)

Largely re-enacted in Employment Protection (Consolidation) Act 1978. Those parts concerning collective matters have now been consolidated into Trade Union and Labour Relations (Consolidation) Act 1992.

35 Employment Protection (Consolidation) Act 1978 (repealed)

Repealed and consolidated into the Employment Rights Act 1996.

36 Employment Rights Act 1996

Repeals and consolidates in part or in whole *inter alia*: Betting, Gaming and Lotteries Act 1963, Race Relations Act 1976, Employment Protection (Consolidation) Act 1978, Education Act 1980, Employment Act 1980, Magistrates' Courts Act 1980, Finance Act 1980, New Towns Act 1981, Civil Aviation Act 1982, Oil and Gas Enterprise Act 1982, Social Security and Housing Benefits Act 1982, Employment Act 1982, Water Act 1983, Reserve Forces (Safeguard of Employment) Act 1985, Local Government Act 1985, Insolvency Act 1985, Housing (Consequential Provisions) Act 1986, Insolvency Act 1986, Wages Act 1986, Social Security Act 1986, Sex Discrimination Act 1986, Income and Corporation Taxes Act 1988, Norfolk and Suffolk Broads Act 1988, Legal Aid Act 1988, Education Reform Act 1988, Housing Act 1988, Dock Work Act 1989, Water Act 1989, Electricity Act 1989, Employment Act 1989, National Health Service and Community Care Act 1990, Employment Act 1990, Environmental Protection Act 1990, Social Security (Consequential Provisions) Act 1992, Further and Higher Education Act 1992, Trade Union and Labour Relations (Consolidation) Act 1992, Trade Union Reform and Employment Rights Act 1993, Pension Schemes Act 1993, Race Relations (Remedies) Act 1994, Social Security (Incapacity for Work) Act 1994, Sunday Trading Act 1994, Deregulation and Contracting Out Act 1994, Health Authorities Act 1995, Environment Act 1995, Pensions Act 1995, Disability Discrimination Act 1995, Reserve Forces Act 1996, Time Off for Public Duties Order 1990, SI 1990/1870, Sex Discrimination and Equal Pay (Remedies) Regulations 1993, SI 1993/2798, Employment Protection (Part-time Employees) Regulations 1995, SI 1995/31, Time Off for Public Duties Order 1995, SI 1995/694, Collective Redundancies and Transfer of Undertakings (Protection of Employment) (Amendment) Regulations 1995, SI 1995/2587, Environment Act 1995 (Consequential Amendments) Regulations 1996, SI 1996/593, Environment Act 1995 (Consequential and Transitional Provisions) (Scotland) Regulations 1996, SI 1996/973.

Amended by Police Act 1997.

36.1 Statement of terms and conditions of employment

Originally ss 1 to 7 EPCA (and s 11 re enforcement) as amended by TURERA. Now ss 1 – 6 ERA (and ss 11 and 12 re enforcement).

(a) *The right*
   (i)   An employee is entitled to be given a written statement of the main terms and conditions of employment within two months of beginning employment (the reduction from three months within which to give the statement to two months was brought about by TURERA). If the employee is going to be sent abroad for a period of more than a month within this initial two-month period, then the statement must be given before he leaves. The employee is entitled to a statement of terms and conditions if his employment is terminated after he has been employed for more than one but less than two months.
   (ii) Certain of the terms must be included in a single document (these are asterisked in the list in (b) below). The facility, allowed by the EPCA, to refer to other documents for these terms was severely curtailed by TURERA.
   (iii) If there are no particulars to be entered under any particular head in the particulars set out in (b) below then this fact must be specified.
(b) *Particulars to be specified*
   (i)   the names of the employer and employee*
   (ii) the date when the employment began*
   (iii) the date on which the employee's period of continuous employment began (taking into account any employment with a previous employer which counts towards that period)*

Items asterisked in the above list must be included in a single document: the 'principal statement' of terms and conditions.

(iv) scale or rate of remuneration or the method of calculating remuneration*
(v) intervals at which remuneration is paid (ie weekly, monthly or other specified intervals)*
(vi) any terms and conditions relating to hours of work (including any terms and conditions relating to normal working hours)*
(vii) any terms and conditions relating to
  - entitlement to holidays, public holidays and holiday pay (the particulars must be sufficient to enable the employee's entitlement, including entitlement to accrued holiday pay on termination of employment, to be calculated)*
  - incapacity for work due to sickness or injury, including any sick pay, and
  - pensions and pension schemes (the requirement to notify this item is excluded in relation to certain pension schemes set up by statute).
(viii) the length of notice required from each party to terminate the employee's employment
(ix) job title or a brief description of the employee's work* (amended by TURERA – previously only job title was allowed)
(x) where the employment is not intended to be permanent, the period for which it is expected to continue or, if it is for a fixed term, the date when it is to end, must be stated (amended by TURERA – previously there was no reference to the period for which a temporary job was expected to last). It should be noted that where the employment is for less than one month then there is no entitlement to a s 1 statement (this was reduced from three months by TURERA)
(xi) the place of work or, if the employee is required or permitted to work at various places, an indication of that fact and of the employer's address* (introduced by TURERA)
(xii) any collective agreements which directly affect the terms and conditions of the employment including, where the employer is not a party, the persons by whom they were made (introduced by TURERA)
(xiii) where the employee is required to work outside the UK for more than one month
  - the period for which he is to work outside the United Kingdom
  - the currency in which his remuneration will be paid whilst working outside the UK
  - any additional remuneration payable/benefits to be provided to or in respect of him, by reason of his being required to work outside the UK, and
  - any terms and conditions relating to his return to the United Kingdom (introduced by TURERA).

Items asterisked in the above list must be included in a single document: the 'principal statement' of terms and conditions.

(c) *Reference to other documents*
   (i)   The section 1 statement may refer the employee for particulars to do with incapacity for work due to sickness or injury, including sick pay provisions, and for details of pensions and pension schemes to another document which is reasonably accessible to the employee.
   (ii) The section 1 statement may refer to the law or to the provisions of any collective agreement directly affecting the employee's terms and conditions which is reasonably accessible to the employee, for the length of notice to be given by either party to terminate his employment.

This very limited facility to refer the employee to other documentation, brought in by TURERA, can be contrasted to the original provisions of the EPCA which allowed the employer to refer the employee to other documents for all the items which had to be notified to him under s 1.

(d) *Note of disciplinary procedure and pensions*
   A section 1 statement must also include:
   (i)   in relation to discipline and grievance
         • a note of any disciplinary rules applicable to the employee (the employee can be referred to another document for this)
         • a note specifying to whom the employee can appeal if he is dissatisfied with any disciplinary decision and how to appeal
         • a note specifying to whom the employee can appeal if he has a grievance and how to deal with this
         • a note of any further steps available in the grievance or disciplinary procedures
         A note relating to discipline and grievance is not required if the employer employs fewer than 20 employees.
   (ii) a note saying whether there is a contracting-out certificate (under the Pension Schemes Act 1993) in force.

(e) *Statement of changes*
   If there are changes in any items of which particulars are required to be given, the employer must give the employee a written statement containing particulars of the change at the earliest opportunity and, in any event, not later than one month after the change in question (or before the employee goes abroad if he is leaving to work outside the UK for more than a month before the statement of changes would otherwise be due).
   Where the employer changes its name or there is a change of employer which does not affect the employee's continuity of employment then that change can be noted in a statement of change rather than a new statement having to be given. If a statement of change is given where there is a change of employer then that statement must also give the employee's original continuity date.

(f) *Enforcement*
   (i)   If the employer does not give an employee a section 1 statement or a

statement of changes of particulars of employment, or gives an incomplete statement, then the employee can ask a tribunal to determine what particulars ought to have been included in the statement.

(ii)   If there is a question regarding the accuracy of the terms in a section 1 statement or in a statement of changes of particulars of employment then either the employer or the employee can refer the matter to a tribunal. The tribunal can confirm or amend the particulars which have been given or substitute other particulars.

(iii)   A claim can be brought at any time up to three months after the employment to which the question relates has finished or, if that is not reasonably practicable, within such further period as is reasonably practicable. (The 'not reasonably practicable' escape clause was inserted by TUR-ERA.)

36.2   Itemised pay statement

Originally ss 8 to 10 EPCA (and s 11 re enforcement) as amended by TURERA. Now ss 8 to 10 ERA (and ss 11 and 12 re enforcement).

(a)   *The right*

An employee is entitled to be given a written itemised pay statement. This must be given either before or at the time he is to be paid and must contain the following information:

(i)   gross pay

(ii)   the amounts of any deductions and the reasons why they have been made. (Where there are fixed deductions which are made from the employee's pay then a separate statement of these can be given to the employee in advance and the global amount of the fixed deductions is then noted on individual pay statements)

(iii)   net pay, and

(iv)   if different parts of the net amount are paid in different ways, the amount and method of payment of each bit.

(b)   *Enforcement*

(i)   If the employee is not given an itemised pay statement or if the statement is incomplete, the employee can refer the matter to a tribunal and the tribunal can decide what particulars ought to have been included in the statement.

(ii)   Where a question arises as to the accuracy of an itemised pay statement or a statement of fixed deductions then either the employer or the employee can refer the matter to a tribunal. A tribunal cannot consider a question solely as to the accuracy of an amount stated in the statement. In other words, the tribunal can look at the reasons for mistakes, but not at the accuracy of the mathematics (although it can consider this under the Protection of Wages provisions – *see 36.3 below*).

(iii) A claim can be brought at any time up to three months after the employee's employment finishes or, if that is not reasonably practicable, within such further period as is practical. (The 'not reasonably practicable' escape clause was inserted by TURERA.)

(iv) If the employee was not given a pay statement or if a pay statement or statement of fixed deductions did not contain the particulars required, the tribunal can make a declaration to that effect and can require the employer to pay the employee a sum not exceeding the amount of all the unnotified deductions which the employer made during the 13 weeks immediately preceding the date when the application to the tribunal was made.

36.3   Protection of Wages – unlawful deductions/payments to employers

Originally contained in the Wages Act 1986. Now ss 13 to 27 ERA. These provisions apply to payments employees make to employers as well as to deductions *per se*.

(a) *Meaning of 'wages'*

Wages are broadly any monetary sums paid by an employer payable by reference to the employee's employment other than items such as repayment of expenses. Both SSP and SMP are deemed to be 'wages' for these purposes.

(b) *Meaning of 'deduction'*

(i) Definition: A 'deduction' is, broadly, any shortfall between the amount which an employee is entitled to receive, after any lawful deductions have been made, and the amount he actually receives.

(ii) Exclusions from the definition of deduction:

- errors of computation
- deductions in respect of overpayment of wages or expenses
- deductions made following any statutory disciplinary procedure
- any requirement on the employer to deduct monies which have been determined to be due to a public authority
- agreed deductions from an employee's wages for the benefit of a third party
- deductions made by the employer in respect of strike or other industrial action taken by an employee
- any amount which the employee has agreed to repay to the employer by deduction from his wages pursuant to a court or tribunal order.

It should be noted that the above items are not necessarily lawful deductions – they are simply excluded from consideration under these particular statutory provisions.

(c) *When deductions are allowable*

For a deduction, which is caught by the Act, to be allowable it must satisfy one of the following criteria. It must either:

(i) be required or authorised by statute; or

(ii) be required or authorised by a provision of the worker's contract – which must have existed at the date when the matter giving rise to the deduction occurred; or

(iii) be a deduction to which the worker has previously signified his written agreement or consent. (Previous consent, in this context, means that consent must be given before the event which gives rise to the deduction being made rather than just pre-dating the deduction itself.)

(d) *Retail employment*

Where an employee is in 'retail employment', then no more than 10 per cent of his gross pay can be deducted from his wages on any pay day, in respect of cash shortages or stock losses. This limit is lifted in respect of wages paid for the employee's final period of employment – where there is no limit on the amount of any such deductions.

(e) *Bringing a claim*

A claim for wrongful deduction may be brought to an industrial tribunal within three months of the deduction complained of.

36.4 Guarantee payments

Originally ss 12 – 18 EPCA, now ss 28 – 35 ERA.

(a) *The right*

(i) Where an employer is unable to provide an employee with work throughout the whole of a day when the employee would normally be working because of either:

- a lack of work of the type which the employee is employed to do; or
- because of any other occurrence affecting the work which the employee is employed to do; then

the employee is entitled to a guarantee payment in respect of that day.

(NB Where the employee's work spans midnight the day on which the employee must be 'workless' is the day in which the greater number of hours are normally worked. If the employee is employed for the same number of hours on both days then it is the second day which must be workless.)

(ii) The amount of a guarantee payment is the employee's daily rate of pay subject to a statutory maximum which is updated from time to time and is currently £14.50p per day. Any contractual pay which the employee is entitled to receive in respect of the same day goes towards discharging the employer's liability to pay a guarantee payment and vice versa.

(iii) The maximum number of days for which guarantee payments can be made in any three-month period is the same as the number of days per week (not exceeding five) which the employee normally works.

(b) *Exclusions from the right to guarantee payments*

(i) Employees who have not had at least one month's continuous service

(ii) Employees employed under:

(a) fixed-term contracts for less than three months; or

(b) to do a specific task which is not expected to take more than three months unless they have been employed for three months

(ii) If the failure to provide work is because of a strike or lock-out

(iv) If the employee unreasonably refuses suitable alternative employment on the day in question; or if he fails to comply with his employer's reasonable requirements to ensure that his services are available on the day in question

(v) Where there is an exemption order, approved by the Secretary of State, in force in respect of the employee.

(c) *Enforcement*

A complaint regarding an employer's failure to pay all or part of an employee's guarantee payment entitlement can be presented to a tribunal within three months' of the employer's failure or, where that is not reasonably practicable, within such further time as is reasonably practicable.

36.5 Sunday working

When Sunday betting was legalised by the Deregulation and Contracting Out Act 1994, statutory protection similar to that in Schedule 4 of the Sunday Trading Act 1994, which covered shop workers was enacted for betting workers by the Deregulation and Contracting Out Act 1994. This Act inserted a new Sch 5A into the Betting, Gaming and Lotteries Act 1963. The Sunday working provisions are now contained in ss 36 to 43, 45, 101, 104, 105(*a*), 108 and 197(2) ERA.

(a) *Who is covered?*

(i) These provisions only apply to those who work in England and Wales.

(ii) A 'betting worker' is a worker in England or Wales who can be required to do work either:

(a) for a bookmaker at a track which includes dealing with betting transactions; or

(b) in a licensed betting office on a day on which the office is open for betting transactions.

(iii) A 'shop worker' is one who can be required to work in or about a shop on a day when the shop is open for serving customers.

(b) *'Protected shop/betting worker'*

(i) A 'protected shop/betting worker' is one who either:

(a) was employed as a shop worker on 26 August 1994 or as a betting worker on 5 January 1995 (the commencement dates of the relevant provisions of the Sunday Trading Act 1994 and the Deregulation and Contracting Out Act 1994), but not to work only on Sundays, and has throughout his service from that date, until the date at which any particular right falls to be determined, continued to be a shop/betting worker; or

(b) one who cannot be required under his contract of employment to work on Sundays (independently of any right to refuse to work on Sundays he may have under the Act).

(ii)   Whilst the employee remains a protected shop worker, however, the employer is entitled not to pay the employee for Sunday work. If there is no specific amount which is referable to the employee's Sunday work then the employer is entitled to reduce the employee's remuneration by the proportion of the week which the employee loses by no longer working on Sundays. If the work is made up during the remainder of the week, then, there will be no loss to the employee in such cases, but employers are entitled to reduce the protected employees' weekly hours by the number of hours which they normally worked on a Sunday.

(iii) A protected employee can only be required to work on Sundays if he has opted in to working on Sundays.

(c) *Opting in*

(i)   A shop/betting worker is not a protected worker if
- he has given his employer an opting-in notice on or after the commencement date of the relevant statute; and
- after giving the notice, he has expressly agreed with his employer to do shop work, or betting work, on Sunday or on a particular Sunday.

(ii)   An 'opting-in notice' is a written notice, signed and dated by the shop/betting worker, in which the worker expressly states that he wishes to work on Sunday or that he does not object to Sunday working.

(d) *Opting out*

(i)   Any shop/betting worker who is not employed purely to work on Sundays, but who, under his contract, may be required to work on Sundays, is entitled to give his employer an opting-out notice. This is so even if the employee opted in to Sunday work.

(ii)   An opting-out notice is a written notice, signed and dated by the employee, saying that the employee objects to Sunday working.

(iii) A shop/betting worker who is entitled to opt out of Sunday working must be given a notice in the following statutory form by his employer:

STATUTORY RIGHTS IN RELATION TO SUNDAY [SHOP/BETTING] WORK

[You have become employed as a shop worker and are or can be required under your contract of employment to do the Sunday work your contract provides for.]

[You have become employed under a contract of employment under which you are or can be required to do Sunday betting work, that is to say, work—

at a track on a Sunday on which your employer is taking bets at the track, or

in a licensed betting office on a Sunday on which it is open for business.]

However, if you wish, you can give notice, as described in the next paragraph, to your employer and you will then have the right not to [work in or about a shop on any Sunday on which the shop is open] [do Sunday betting work on any Sunday] once three months have passed from the date on which you gave notice.

Your notice must—

be in writing;

be signed and dated by you;

say that you object to [Sunday working][doing Sunday betting work].

For three months after you give the notice, your employer can still require you to do all the Sunday work your contract provides for. After the three-month period has ended, you have the right to complain to an industrial tribunal if, because of your refusal to [work on Sundays on which the shop is open] [do Sunday betting work], your employer—

dismisses you, or

does something else detrimental to you, for example, failing to promote you.

Once you have the rights described, you can surrender them only by giving your employer a further notice, signed and dated by you, saying that you wish to [work on Sunday] [do Sunday betting work] or that you do not object to [Sunday working] [doing Sunday betting work] and then agreeing with your employer to [work on Sundays] [do such work on Sundays] or on a particular Sunday.

    (iv)   The above statement must be given to the employee within two months of the employee becoming an eligible shop/betting worker. If the employer fails to provide the statutory statement within two months then the three months' notice period during which the employee can normally be required to continue to work on Sundays is reduced to one month. This does not apply if the employee gives an opting-out notice before the two-month period for giving the statement expires.

    (v)   An employee who opts out of Sunday working can still be required to work on Sundays during the three months' (or one month – *see iv above*) statutory notice period before his opt-out takes effect.

    (vi)   Where an employee has opted out of Sunday work then he can still opt back in again but, unless he does, any contractual requirement for Sunday work becomes unenforceable after the end of the notice period.

(e) *The rights*

    (i)   Dismissal for refusal to work on Sunday

        • A protected or opted-out shop/betting worker is to be regarded as having been unfairly dismissed if the principal reason for dismissal is that he

            • refused, or proposed to refuse, to work on Sundays or a particular Sunday (provided that the Sunday in question is not during the

notice period after the opting-out certificate has been given, but before it takes effect); or
  - gave, or proposed to give, an opting-out notice to the employer.
  - There is no minimum qualifying period of employment before the employee is entitled to bring such cases.

(ii) Selection for redundancy for refusal to work on Sunday
  - A protected or opted-out shop/betting worker is to be regarded as having been unfairly dismissed if:
    - the principal reason for dismissal is redundancy
    - there are others holding similar positions who have not been dismissed; and
    - the principal reason for his selection for dismissal was that he
      - refused, or proposed to refuse, to work on Sundays or a particular Sunday (provided that the Sunday in question is not during the notice period after the opting-out certificate has been given, but before it takes effect); or
      - gave, or proposed to give, an opting-out notice to the employer.
  - There is no minimum qualifying period of employment before the employee is entitled to bring such cases.

(iii) Right not to be subjected to a detriment for refusal to work on Sunday
  - A protected or opted-out shop/betting worker has the right not to be subjected to any detriment by his employer because the employee
    - refused, or proposed to refuse, to work on Sundays or on a particular Sunday (other than a Sunday during the notice period after an opting-out certificate has been given to an employer, but before it takes effect); or
    - gave, or proposed to give, an opting-out notice to the employer.
  - These provisions do not apply where the detriment in question is the employee's dismissal, where the employee will have to claim unfair dismissal rather than a detriment. A detriment for these purposes includes any act, or deliberate failure to act, by the employer.
  - None of the following can amount to a detriment for these purposes:
    - failure to pay the employee or to provide benefits in respect of Sunday work he has not done
    - failure to provide the employee with work where the employer is statutorily allowed not to provide work (where a protected worker was obliged to work on Sunday but now does not, the employer is not obliged to provide alternative work or remuneration in lieu)
    - the employer can offer to pay other protected or opted-out employees a premium for working on Sunday without either the failure to pay or the failure to offer the work being a detriment to anyone who is not made this offer
    - the employer can offer to pay a protected or opted-out employee a

premium for working on Sunday without either the failure to pay or the failure to offer being a detriment to anyone who refuses the offer.
- Where an action continues over a period it is the beginning of that period which is relevant for deciding when that action occurred.
- A deliberate failure to act is treated as having been done when it was either decided on or when the employer does an act inconsistent with the act he has failed to do.

(iv) *Dismissal for asserting a statutory right*
If an employee is dismissed for having brought a claim against the employer under these provisions then, provided:

- that the claim was brought in good faith, regardless of the merits of the claim, and
- the employee made it clear in general terms what he was claiming;

the dismissal will be considered to be unfair.

36.6   Protection for health and safety representatives, trustees of pension schemes and employee representatives

(a) *Health and safety representatives*
Protection for health and safety representatives was originally introduced by Sch 5 of TURERA to comply with the employment protection aspects of the Health and Safety European 'Framework Directive' (Directive 89/391/EEC). These rights were introduced by way of amendments to the EPCA mainly in: ss 22A to C, 57A and 59 – now ss 44, 48, 49, 100, 105, 108, 109 ERA and 117, 120, 125, 128, 130 and 132 ERA re remedies. These provisions were amended by the Health and Safety (Consultation with Employees) Regulations 1996 (SI 1996 No. 1513).

(i)   To whom and in what circumstances is protection afforded?
- Anyone designated by the employer to do anything connected with reducing or preventing health and safety risks, where the action taken by the employer is because they did anything to reduce or prevent a risk, or proposed to.
- Health and safety representatives and members of Safety Committees, who are either designated as such or who are acknowledged as such by the employer (under the Safety Representatives and Safety Committees Regulations 1977 SI 1977 No. 500 – SRSCR) and representatives of employee safety appointed under the Health and Safety (Consultation with Employees) Regulations 1996 SI 1996 No. 1513 – HSCER. Health and safety representatives and members of Safety Committees can be appointed, under SRSCR, where trades unions are recognised by the employer. Representatives of employee safety can be appointed under HSCER where no union is recognised.
- An employee who has action taken against him because he has

brought something which he reasonably believes to be harmful or potentially harmful to health and safety to his employer's attention.

An action in this type of case is only available where there are either no health and safety representatives or safety committees, or where it is not reasonably practicable for the employee to raise the matter through a safety representative or committee.

- An employee who has action taken against him because he left or proposed to leave, or refused to return to his place of work, or a dangerous part of it, because he reasonably believed there to be a serious and imminent danger which he could not have been expected to avert.
- An employee who has action taken against him because he took, or proposed to take, appropriate steps to protect himself or others in circumstances of danger which he reasonably believed to be serious and imminent.

In judging whether the steps the employee took were appropriate all the circumstances of the case must be looked at, including the employee's knowledge and the facilities and advice available to the employee. The employee loses his protection under this provision if the employer is able to show that the steps that the employee took were so negligent that the employer's treatment of him was reasonable in the circumstances.

(ii) Rights

- Not to suffer a detriment by any deliberate act or inaction on the part of the employer.
- Dismissal for any of the above reasons is automatically unfair, as is selection for redundancy for those reasons where there are others holding similar positions who have not been dismissed. There is no qualifying period for entitlement to claim unfair dismissal, nor is there an upper age cut-off for entitlement to claim.

(iii) Remedies

A complaint must be brought within three months of the action complained of.

Detriment

- It is for the employer to show the reason for any action or failure to act.
- If the tribunal is satisfied that the employee has been treated detrimentally then the tribunal will make a declaration to that effect and award such compensation as is just and equitable.

Dismissal

- Where the employee has been designated by the employer to look after health and safety matters, is a health and safety representative or a member of a safety committee, then:

- a special minimum basic award is available, currently £2,770, as well as a 'special award' which is the same as the special award originally introduced by the Employment Act 1982 for trade union dismissals (for more details of special compensation see 36.12(d) below).
- A 'special' compensatory award is also provided for. Where the employee has asked for reinstatement or re-engagement (except where the tribunal finds that the principal reason for dismissal was redundancy). The amount of the special award is:

1. Where the tribunal decided to make no order for reinstatement or re-engagement:
   One week's pay × 104 or £13,775 whichever is the greater (subject to a maximum of £27,500) (NB The statutory limit of a week's pay does not count for these purposes.)
2. Where the employer has failed to comply with an order for reinstatement or re-engagement:
   One week's pay × 156 or £20,600 whichever is the greater.

There is no upper maximum.

But:
- if the applicant is over 64 then the special award is to be reduced by 1/12 for each month over 64
- the special award can be reduced because of the employee's misconduct before dismissal, as the tribunal finds just and equitable
- the fact that an employer has recruited a permanent replacement for the dismissed employee can only be taken into account if he can show that it was not reasonably practicable for him to arrange to have the applicant's work done without engaging a replacement.
- Interim relief can be sought from the tribunal. Where interim relief is granted it has the effect of continuing the employee's employment either by way of reinstatement or re-engagement on acceptable terms, until the hearing of the unfair dismissal claim.

(b) *Trustees of occupational pension schemes*
The rights and protection for trustees of occupational pension schemes were originally introduced by ss 42 to 46 of the Pensions Act 1995. These rights were introduced by way of amendments to the EPCA mainly in: ss 22A to C, 31A, 57, 57A, 59, 64, 71(2A and B), 72, 73, 75A and 77 to 79. These provisions are now ss 44, 48, 49, 58 to 60, 98(6), 100, 105, 108, 109, 117 to 122, 125, 128, 130 and 132 ERA.
  (i)   Right not to suffer a detriment or to be dismissed
- Employee trustees of occupational pension schemes related to their employment are entitled not to have any detrimental action taken against them by their employer (including any deliberate inaction), because they performed or proposed to perform any duties as trustees.

- The dismissal of employee trustees of occupational pension schemes or their selection for redundancy on those grounds (where there are others holding similar positions who have not been dismissed) will be automatically unfair and will attract special basic and compensatory awards (*see under* **Health and safety representatives** *above*). There is no qualifying period for entitlement to claim unfair dismissal on these grounds.

  The general pattern of this protection is similar to the protection afforded in the case of health and safety representatives (*see (a) above*)

(ii) Right to time off for occupational pension scheme trustees

- Employee occupational pension scheme trustees are entitled to be permitted reasonable paid time off:
  - to carry out their duties as trustees; or
  - for training relevant to their duties as trustees.
- The employee is entitled to be paid for time off under this provision as if he had been at work normally.
- The employee can complain to an industrial tribunal if he is either refused time off or is not paid, or paid fully, for it.

(c) *Employee representatives*

The Collective Redundancies and Transfers of Undertaking (Protection of Employment) Regulations 1995 SI 1995/2587 introduced a new concept of elected 'Employee Representatives' who the employer must consult on collective redundancies (*see* TULRA) and proposed transfers of undertakings (*see Transfer of Undertakings (Protection of Employment) Regulations 1981*) where no trade union is recognised. The regulations originally added protection for employee representatives into the EPCA by adding ss 22AA, 31AA and 57AA and making various amendments to other parts of the EPCA. These changes have now become ss 47, 61 to 63, 103, 105(6) ERA.

(i) Right not to suffer a detriment or to be dismissed

- An employee representative, or someone who is a candidate to become an employee representative is entitled not to suffer a detriment because of anything which is done by them in carrying out their duties in respect of consultation with the employer either under TULRA or TOUR or as a candidate for election as an employee representative.
- The dismissal of employee representatives or their selection for redundancy on those grounds (where there are others holding similar positions who have not been dismissed) will be automatically unfair and will attract special basic and compensatory awards. There is no qualifying period for entitlement to claim unfair dismissal on these grounds.
- The general pattern of this protection is similar to the protection afforded in the case of health and safety representatives (*see (a) above*).

(ii) Right to time off
Employee representatives and candidates for election as employee representatives are entitled to be permitted reasonable paid time off:
- to carry out their duties as employee representatives; or
- in connection with their candidacy.

The employee can complain to an industrial tribunal if he is either refused time off or is not paid, or paid fully, for it.

36.7 Time off for public duties

Originally s 29 EPCA (and s 30 re enforcement). Now ss 50 ERA (and s 51 re enforcement).
(i) JPs are entitled to time off to perform any of the duties of their office.
(ii) Members of
- local authorities
- statutory tribunals
- police authorities including the Service Authority for National Criminal Intelligence Service and the Service Authority for the Crime Squad (this extended meaning of 'police authority' was brought in by the Police Act 1997)
- boards of prison visitors or prison visiting committees
- certain health bodies
- certain education bodies
- the Environment Agency or the Scottish Environment Protection Agency

are allowed to have time off to attend meetings of the body (including committees and sub-committees) and to do anything else for the purpose of discharging the functions of the body in question or its committees.
(iii) The amount of time which an employee is allowed is what is reasonable and depends *inter alia* on:
- the amount of time off which an employee has for trade-union activities and duties;
- the amount of time off required for the public duties in question; and
- the needs of the employer's business.
(iv) Time off under this provision is unpaid.

36.8 Suspension on medical grounds

Originally ss 19 to 22 EPCA. Now ss 64, 65 and 69 ERA (and s 70 re enforcement).
(a) *Who is entitled*
An employee who is suspended because of a requirement imposed by
(i) Regulation 16 of the Control of Lead at Work Regulations 1980
(ii) Regulation 16 of the Ionising Radiation Regulations 1985; or
(iii) Regulation 11 of the Control of Substances Hazardous to Health Regulations 1988.

(b) *The rights*
  (i)   The employee is entitled to be paid his normal remuneration for up to 26 weeks.
  (ii) An employee who is dismissed because of a requirement to suspend him on medical grounds can claim unfair dismissal if he had one month's continuous service before the date of dismissal.
  (iii) Where an employer dismisses a replacement who has been hired to cover for such an employee then provided
    • that the employer informed the replacement in writing that he was being hired to cover for someone on medical suspension and would be dismissed when that person returned; and
    • the employer dismisses the replacement to take the suspended employee back

    then the employer will be deemed to have a 'substantial' reason for dismissal. The employer will still have to satisfy the tribunal that it acted reasonably in dismissing the replacement in the circumstances.

(c) *Exclusions from the right to remuneration*
  The following are excluded from entitlement to remuneration whilst under medical suspension:
  (i)   those who have been continuously employed for less than one month before being suspended
  (ii) those on a fixed-term contract of three months' or less, provided they have not been employed for more than three months
  (iii) those hired for a job which is expected to take three months or less, provided they have not been employed for more than three months
  (iv) an employee who is sick
  (v)   an employee who unreasonably refuses to undertake suitable alternative employment
  (vi) an employee who unreasonably refuses to comply with the employer's reasonable requirements for keeping his services available.

36.9   Rights connected with pregnancy and maternity

(a) *Time off for ante-natal care*
  Introduced by the Employment Act 1980, originally adding a new s 31A to the EPCA. These provisions are now contained in ss 55 to 57 ERA.
  (i)   An employee who is pregnant and who has made an appointment to attend for ante-natal care on the advice of a medical practitioner, midwife or health visitor is entitled to take paid time off during working hours to keep the appointment
  (ii) Except for the first ante-natal appointment, the employee must show the employer, if he asks for it:
    • a certificate from a medical practitioner, midwife or health visitor to say that she is pregnant; and

- an appointment card or document showing that an ante-natal appointment has been made.

(iii) An employee can complain to an industrial tribunal that she has
- unreasonably been refused time off; or
- that her employer has refused to pay her fully or at all for the time she has taken off for ante-natal care.

(iv) If a tribunal finds that a woman has been unreasonably refused time off, then, as well as declaring that to be the case, it must also award the woman the remuneration which the employer would have paid her if she had not been refused the time off.

(b) *Suspension on maternity grounds*

The right to payment on suspension on maternity grounds was added to the EPCA by TURERA as ss 45 to 47 EPCA. The provisions are now contained in ss 66 to 70 ERA.

(i) An employee is suspended on maternity grounds if she is suspended pursuant to an Order specified under s 66(2) ERA on the ground that she is pregnant, has recently given birth or is breast-feeding a child. Currently there is one Order made under this provision: Suspension From Work (On Maternity Grounds) Order 1994 (SI 1994/2930) which in turn refers to a list of reasons for suspension under this heading. The reasons for suspension are contained in Regs 13A and 13B Management of Health and Safety at Work Regulations 1992 (SI 1992/2051) (introduced by the Management of Health and Safety at Work (Amendment) Regulations 1994 (SI 1994/2865) and in Annexes 1 and 2 of EC Directive 92/85/EEC – the Pregnant Workers Directive.

(ii) As an alternative to suspension the employee has a right to be offered any alternative employment which the employer has available. For alternative employment to be 'suitable' for these purposes it must be
- suitable in relation to the employee
- appropriate for her to do in the circumstances; and
- on terms and conditions not substantially less favourable than her existing terms and conditions.

(iii) An employee is entitled to be paid whilst she is suspended on maternity grounds. Any contractual payment made by the employer goes towards discharging the employer's liability to pay the woman whilst on suspension so that if the employee does any work for the employer, the remuneration due to her on suspension will 'top up' her pay to the extent that it is less than her normal 'week's pay'.

(iv) It should be noted that if an employee is dismissed in circumstances where she ought to be suspended under these provisions, she will be able to claim that her dismissal is automatically unfair. It will also be automatically unfair to select a woman for redundancy because of her entitlement to be suspended because of pregnancy where there are others holding similar positions who have not been dismissed.

(c) *Right to maternity leave for all employees*

A general right to maternity leave, for all women regardless of service, was introduced by TURERA. The purpose of this was to give effect to the Pregnant Workers' Directive 92/85/EEC. TURERA gave effect to these changes by inserting new ss 33 to 38A into the EPCA. The provisions are now contained in ss 71 to 78 ERA.

(i) The right

There is a general right for employees to have 14 weeks' maternity leave regardless of the length of time for which they have been employed by their employer provided that they comply with all the notification requirements. Where an employee has a contractual right to maternity leave then she can pick-and-mix her contractual and statutory rights to give herself the best composite right.

(ii) Notification requirements

- At least 21 days before her Maternity Leave Period (MLP) commences the employee must inform her employer:
  - that she is pregnant
  - the expected week of childbirth (EWC) (or, if childbirth has already occurred, the date on which it occurred)
  - of a date, no earlier than the beginning of the 11th week before the EWC when the employee intends her absence to begin. But
    - where the employee's first day of absence for her MLP is the first day after the beginning of the sixth week before EWC, the employee need not give advance notice of her intended absence, but must inform the employer as soon as is reasonably practicable that she is away from work due to pregnancy
    - where the employee's MLP begins on the day of childbirth she need only inform her employer as soon as is reasonably practicable after the birth that she has given birth.
- Notification of absence or intended absence must be in writing if the employer so requests.
- If the employee is entitled, and wishes, to exercise her right to return later than the end of the MLP, within 29 weeks of the week of childbirth, then she must also inform her employer that she intends to exercise that right. (For the right to return after the MLP for those with more than two years' service at the 11th week before EWC *see (d) below*.)
- If the employer asks her to, the employee must provide a certificate from a doctor or midwife stating the EWC.

(iii) Commencement of maternity leave period

The MLP commences with whichever is the first of the following events:

- the date at which the employee has notified her employer that her MLP will begin
- the first day after the beginning of the sixth week before the EWC on which she is absent from work wholly or partly because of pregnancy
- in any other case the date of childbirth.

(iv) Continuation of contract

An employee who has fulfilled the notification requirements and who is absent from work during her MLP is entitled to the terms and conditions of her employment, other than remuneration, as if she was not absent and had not been pregnant or given birth to a child.

(v) Duration of the MLP

The MLP lasts for 14 weeks from its commencement or until at least two weeks after the birth of the child if later (the ban on an employee working within two weeks starting with the date of childbirth was introduced by Maternity (Compulsory Leave) Regulations 1994 (SI 1994/2479)).

(vi) Return after maternity leave

An employee who wants to return to work before the end of her MLP must give her employer at least seven days' notice of her proposed return date. If the employee tries to return without giving seven days' notice the employer can postpone her return so that he effectively has seven days' notice of her return. This is subject to a proviso that the employer cannot postpone the employee's return beyond the end of her 14 weeks' MLP.

(vii) Redundancy during the maternity leave period

If there is a redundancy during the maternity leave period then the employee is entitled to be offered any suitable alternative employment which is available on terms and conditions which are not substantially less beneficial than those she enjoyed under her previous contract.

If the employer fails to offer suitable alternative employment which is available or if the employee is selected for redundancy because of any reason connected with her pregnancy or maternity leave (where there are others holding similar positions who have not been dismissed), the employee will be automatically treated as having been unfairly dismissed. If an employee has a right to return within 29 weeks of the birth and is either unfairly dismissed or made redundant, during or at the end of her MLP, then it is a condition of entitlement to exercise her right to return that she repays the employer any unfair dismissal compensation or redundancy payment paid, if he asks her to.

(d) *Right to return to work after extended maternity leave*

The right to maternity leave in the EPCA, for employees with more than two years' service, was significantly amended by TURERA and new ss 39 to 44 were substituted in EPCA. These provisions are now contained in ss 79 to 85 ERA.

(i)   The right
  • The 'right to return' is the right of an employee to return to work at any
    time from the end of her Maternity Leave Period (MLP) up to 29 weeks
    after the beginning of the week in which childbirth occurs.
  • To be entitled to this 'right to return' the employee must:
    • fulfil the requirements to be entitled to maternity leave *(see (c)*
      above)
    • have notified her employer that she intends to exercise her right to
      return to work; and
    • at the beginning of the 11th week before the expected week of child-
      birth (EWC) she must have been continuously employed for at least
      two years.
  • Where the employee has a contractual right to return then she can
    pick-and-mix her contractual and statutory rights to give herself the
    best composite right.
(ii)   Notification requirements
  • As well as fulfilling the notification requirements before the start of her
    MLP *(see (c) (ii) above)*, the employer can ask for written confirmation
    that the employee still wishes to exercise her right to return.
    Such a request:
    • cannot be made earlier than 21 days before the end of the MLP
    • must be in writing;
    • must state that if the employee does not answer the request within
      14 days, or if that is not reasonably practicable, within such further
      time as is reasonably practicable, she will lose her right to return.
  • The employee must give 21 days' written notice of her intended return
    date.
(iii) Postponing the return
  • The employer may postpone the employee's return for up to four
    weeks after the notified day of return (NDR) if he notifies the em-
    ployee:
    • of the specific reason for delaying her return; and
    • the date, not more than four weeks after the NDR, when the em-
      ployee can return to work.
  • An employee unable to return owing to sickness can postpone her re-
    turn for up to four weeks after her NDR (or after the 29-week period if
    no NDR has been notified):
    • she must provide her employer with a medical certificate before the
      NDR (or the end of the 29-week period if no NDR)
    • the certificate must specify that she is unable to return due to illness
    • this right to delay can only be exercised once.
  • Where there is an interruption of work, due to industrial action or
    otherwise, such that it is not reasonable to expect the employee to re-
    turn at her NDR or at the end of the 29-week period:

- if the employee has notified her intended return date, she may return when work resumes or as soon as is reasonably practicable afterwards
- if the employee has not notified her intended return date, she may exercise her right to return so that she returns within 28 days of the end of the interruption of work.

(iv) Return to what?

The employee's primary right to return is a right to return to work

- with
  - the employer by whom she was employed at the end of her MLP; or
  - his successor
- in the job in which she was employed before she went on maternity leave
  - on terms and conditions as to remuneration no less favourable than if she had not been absent
  - with seniority, pension and similar rights as if her employment up to the end of her MLP was continuous with her employment after her return (subject to credits in certain cases under Social Security Act 1989 schedule 5)
  - otherwise on terms and conditions as if she had not been absent after her maternity leave period.

(v) Redundancy before return date

- If it is not reasonably practicable by reason of redundancy to permit the employee to return to work, she is entitled to be offered any suitable alternative employment which is available on terms and conditions which are not substantially less beneficial than those she enjoyed under her previous contract.
- If the employer:
  - fails to offer suitable alternative employment which is available; or
  - selects an employee for redundancy for any reason connected with pregnancy or childbirth, where there are others holding similar positions who have not been dismissed

the employee will be treated as having been automatically unfairly dismissed.

- If an employee has a right to return within 29 weeks of the birth and is either unfairly dismissed or made redundant, during or at the end of her MLP, then it is a condition of her entitlement to exercise her right to return that she repays the employer any unfair dismissal compensation or redundancy payment paid, if he asks her to.

(vi) Failure to permit a woman to return after maternity leave and dismissal

These provisions were originally contained in s 56 EPCA. The Employment Act 1980 made major amendments adding s 56A to the EPCA. TURERA made further minor amendments. These provisions are now contained in s 96 ERA.

- Where a woman is not allowed to return to work after extended maternity leave (assuming she has satisfied all the notification requirements), then she is, *prima facie*, treated as having been dismissed for the reason for which she was not allowed to return to work; and she is treated as having been employed up to her NRD.
- There are two exceptions to this general position:
  - Where the employer employs five or fewer employees immediately before the end of her MLP (including any employees employed by any associated employers).

    If in such cases it is not reasonably practicable for the employer (or his successor):
    - to offer suitable alternative employment; or
    - to allow the woman to return to her original job

    then the woman will not be treated as having been dismissed.
  - If it is not reasonably practicable, for a reason other than redundancy, for the woman to be allowed to return to her original job and
    - the employer or a successor of his offers the woman suitable alternative employment and
    - she accepts or unreasonably refuses that offer

    then, again, the woman will not be treated as having been dismissed by being refused the right to return to work.

(e) *Dismissal of a temporary replacement*

This was originally contained in s 61 EPCA, was subject to minor amendment by TURERA, and is now contained in s 106 ERA.

Where a temporary replacement is engaged to do the work of an employee who is:

- suspended on maternity grounds; or
- absent because of pregnancy or confinement

then, provided:

- the replacement is informed of this fact when they take the job on; and
- the replacement is dismissed to allow for the woman to return to work

then the employer will be seen to have a substantial reason for dismissing the employee for unfair dismissal purposes. The employer will still have to show, of course, that it acted fairly in treating that reason as a sufficient reason for dismissal.

(f) *Right not to be dismissed because of pregnancy or childbirth*

A limited right in the EPCA, making dismissal for pregnancy automatically unfair in certain circumstances, was amended by TURERA which inserted a new s 60 into the EPCA. This right is now contained in s 99 ERA.

An employee is considered to be automatically unfairly dismissed if she is dismissed:

- for any reason related to her pregnancy
- where her MLP is ended by dismissal for any reason connected with
  - the fact that she has given birth to a child; or
  - the fact that she took maternity leave or the benefits attached to it

- when she ought to have been suspended on maternity grounds
- where her MLP (or extended maternity period) is ended by dismissal because of redundancy and she was not offered suitable alternative employment which was available; or
- where she is ill at the end of her maternity leave, has given the employer a medical certificate covering the period of her illness (up to four weeks) and she is dismissed during the currency of the medical certificate.

(g) *Right to pay in lieu of notice whilst absent due to the pregnancy or maternity*
Employees who are given notice when they are away from work due to pregnancy or confinement are entitled to be paid in lieu of notice provided that their notice entitlement is not over a week more than the statutory minimum notice entitlement.

Any sick pay, SSP, maternity pay, SMP or holiday pay goes towards discharging the employer's obligations as do State sickness benefits.

Where it was the employee who gave notice, the requirement for the employer to pay for the notice period in such cases only applies if the employee actually leaves the employer's employment.

(h) *Automatic right to written reasons for dismissal in pregnancy and maternity cases*
This provision became s 53(2A) EPCA by an amendment made by TURERA and is now s 92(4) ERA.

A woman who is dismissed while pregnant or in trying to exercise her right to return to work is entitled to be given written reasons for dismissal without asking for them.

36.10   Notice rights

Originally contained in ss 49 to 52 and Schedule 3 EPCA, Social Security and Housing Benefits Act 1982, Social Security (Incapacity for Work) Act 1994 and TURERA. These are now contained in ss 86 to 91 ERA.

(a) *General right*
  (i)   Employees who have been employed for more than four weeks and less than two years are entitled to a minimum of one week's notice to terminate their contracts of employment. After completing two years' continuous employment an employee is entitled to a minimum of two weeks' notice with an extra week per completed year of service up to 12 weeks' after 12 completed years of service.
  (ii) Employees who have been employed for more than four weeks must give a minimum of one week's notice to terminate their contracts of employment.

(b) *Right to pay in lieu of notice*
  (i)   An employee who gives or who is given notice and who
        - is ready and willing to work, but is not given any work by his employer
        - is incapable of work because of sickness or injury
        - is absent from work wholly or partly because of pregnancy or childbirth, or

- is absent from work on holiday

is entitled to be paid in lieu of notice provided that their notice entitlement is not over a week more than the statutory minimum notice entitlement.

(ii) Any sick pay, SSP, maternity pay, SMP or holiday pay goes towards discharging the employer's obligations as do State sickness benefits. If the employee gives notice of termination then the requirement for the employer to pay for the notice period in such cases only applies if the employee actually leaves the employer's employment.

(iii) The right to be paid in lieu of notice ceases if, and when, an employee is guilty of gross misconduct and could therefore be summarily dismissed or if the employee takes part in a strike.

36.11 Written reasons for dismissal

Previously s 53 EPCA as extended by TURERA in respect of pregnant women and those dismissed on maternity leave – now s 92 ERA.

(a) *General right*
   (i)   An employee who has been employed for not less than two years before being dismissed is entitled to request written reasons for dismissal.
   (ii) Where such a request is made the employer must provide written reasons within 14 days of the request.

(b) *Pregnancy and childbirth*
An employee who is pregnant when dismissed or whose Maternity Leave Period ends by reason of dismissal is entitled to be provided with written reasons for dismissal automatically.

36.12 Unfair dismissal

Provisions concerning unfair dismissal are derived from: Betting Gaming and Lotteries Act 1963, EPCA, Employment Acts 1980, 1982 and 1989, Sex Discrimination Act 1986, TURERA, Sunday Trading Act 1994, Deregulation and Contracting Out Act 1994, TULRA, Collective Redundancies and Transfer of Undertakings (Protection of Employment)(Amendment) Regulations 1995 (SI 1995/2587), Pensions Act 1995. These rights are now contained in:

- ss 94 to 110 dealing with qualification to claim and the circumstances in which an unfair dismissal claim can be brought
- ss 111 to 134 dealing with bringing an unfair dismissal claim and remedies for unfair dismissal.

(a) *General right*
   (i)   Entitlement to claim
        There is a general right for employees not to be unfairly dismissed. To be entitled to claim unfair dismissal the employee:
        - must have more than two years' continuous service (must be under 'normal retirement age' for an employee in that organisation or if there is no normal retirement age, under 65)

- must be normally employed to work in Great Britain
- must not be employed under a fixed-term contract with a valid exclusion against claiming unfair dismissal
- must not be dismissed whilst taking part in industrial action
- must be 'dismissed'. A dismissal occurs where:
  - an employee is dismissed with or without notice
  - a fixed-term contract expires without being renewed on the same terms
  - an employee is 'constructively dismissed' – ie he is entitled to leave because the employer fundamentally breaches his contract of employment
  - an employee who is under notice gives counter-notice to the employer which expires earlier than the employer's original notice.

(ii) The elements of unfair dismissal
Where there is an unfair dismissal claim it is for the employer to show the tribunal:

- the principal reason for dismissing the employee
- that the reason for dismissal was one of the following
  - related to the employee's capability or qualifications to do the work for which he was employed
  - related to the employee's conduct
  - the employee was redundant, or
  - there was a statutory bar on the employee continuing to work in the position which he held

or the reason was some other substantial reason which would justify the dismissal of an employee holding the position which that employee held.

It is then for the tribunal to decide (rather than the onus being on either party to satisfy it) that the employer acted fairly in dismissing the employee for that reason.

In determining:

- what the principal reason for dismissal was
- whether it was a sufficient reason to justify the dismissal of the employee; or
- whether the dismissal was fair or not

no account is to be taken of any pressure exerted on the employer by way of industrial action or threatened industrial action.

(b) *Special cases*

(i) Failure to allow a woman to return after maternity leave
This is dealt with under maternity rights. It applies to cases where a woman who has a right to return to work after extended maternity leave (ie the right to return within 29 weeks of the birth of her child) is not allowed to return to work. In such cases she is treated as having been dismissed on her notified return date.

Where the employee is dismissed in a redundancy situation without being offered alternative work which is available then her dismissal is automatically unfair.

In other cases the fairness of the dismissal must be judged by considering whether the employer would have been acting reasonably or unreasonably in treating [the reason for dismissal] as a sufficient reason for dismissing the employee if she had not been absent from work. It should be noted that the dismissal of a temporary replacement for a woman who has been on maternity leave or who is suspended on maternity grounds is deemed to be for a substantial reason provided:

- that the person was told in writing that they were going to be a temporary replacement; and
- the person is dismissed so that the woman can resume work.

(The employer will still have to show that the dismissal of the temporary replacement was fair in all the circumstances of the case.)

(ii) Dismissal related to pregnancy or childbirth

An employee is considered to be automatically unfairly dismissed if she is dismissed for reasons related to pregnancy or childbirth or having taken maternity leave. (*See mainly under rights connected with pregnancy and maternity above.*)

(iii) Dismissal in health and safety cases

Employees who are dismissed because:

- they are health and safety representatives
- they are representatives of employee safety
- they are members of a health and safety committee
- they have brought a health and safety issue to the employer's notice
- they have taken steps to protect themselves or others; or
- they have left work where they perceive a serious danger to health and safety

are treated as having been automatically unfairly dismissed. (*See also rights of health and safety representatives above.*)

(iv) Shop workers/betting workers

Shop or betting workers who are dismissed for refusing to work on a Sunday or Sundays or for giving or proposing to give their employer an opting-out certificate are considered to be automatically unfairly dismissed (*see mainly under Sunday working – 36.5 above*).

(v) Pension scheme trustees

Employees who are trustees of the occupational pension scheme who are dismissed for being trustees or for undertaking any of the duties as such are considered to be automatically unfairly dismissed (*see mainly under Trustees of occupational pension schemes – 36.6(b)above*).

(vi) Employee representatives

Employees who are dismissed for being employee representatives (ie those elected for purposes of being consulted in relation to proposed redundancies or the transfer of an undertaking) or for standing for election as employee representatives are considered to be automatically unfairly dismissed *(see mainly under Employee representatives – 36.6(c) above)*

(vii) Assertion of a statutory right
- An employee who is dismissed because:
  - he brought proceedings to enforce a relevant statutory right of his against the employer; or
  - alleged that the employer had infringed a relevant statutory right of his
  is considered to be automatically unfairly dismissed. It does not matter for these purposes
    - whether the employee actually has that statutory right or if it has been infringed provided that the claim is made in good faith
    - if a specific claim is not made – provided it is reasonably clear to the employer what right it is being claimed was infringed.
- The relevant statutory rights are:
  - any right under the ERA whose remedy is by way of complaint to an industrial tribunal
  - a claim for minimum notice
  - the right not to have unauthorised deductions of TU subscriptions or contributions to the union's political fund made
  - action short of dismissal for trade-union membership
  - time off for trade-union duties or activities or payment for time off for trade-union duties

(viii) Selection for redundancy for certain reasons
- Where an employee is selected for redundancy in circumstances where the redundancy applies to other employees who have not been dismissed; and
- the reason for selection is one of a number of unacceptable reasons
then the employee's dismissal is automatically unfair.

The unacceptable reasons for these purposes are, broadly, those set out in paragraphs i to vii above:
- the employee was selected for redundancy because of a reason related to maternity or pregnancy
- the employee was selected for redundancy for health and safety reasons
- the employee was a shop or betting worker and was selected for redundancy for a reason related to not wishing to work on Sundays
- the employee was a trustee of an occupational pension scheme and was selected for redundancy for a reason related to carrying out his duties in respect of the scheme
- the employee was an employee representative or seeking election as such and was selected for redundancy for a reason related to carrying out his duties as an employee representative or in connection with seeking election

- the employee was selected for redundancy because he had asserted a relevant statutory right against his employer.

(c) *Complaint to a tribunal*

An employee may present an unfair dismissal complaint to an industrial tribunal within three months of the date of dismissal or, if that is not reasonably practicable, within such further time as the tribunal considers to be reasonably practicable.

(d) *Remedies*

    (i)   Reinstatement and re-engagement

If a tribunal finds that an unfair dismissal complaint is made out then it must explain to the employee the orders which it can make for reinstatement and re-engagement and ask the employee if he or she wishes the tribunal to make such an order.

- Reinstatement – an order for reinstatement is that the employee be put back into the position in which he would have been if he had not been dismissed.
- Re-engagement – an order for re-engagement is that the employee be put into a different job to that from which he was dismissed. In the case of re-engagement the tribunal will set out the terms on which the employee is to be re-engaged.
- If the employer unreasonably fails to comply with an order for reinstatement or re-engagement then the tribunal will award compensation. The amount which is awarded can be increased by an additional award which will be:
  - in a case where the dismissal amounted to unlawful sex or race discrimination – an extra 26 to 52 weeks' pay; and
  - in any other case – an extra 13 to 26 weeks' pay

An additional award cannot be made where the employee is entitled to a 'Special' basic and compensatory award.

    (ii)   Compensation

Compensation is broadly of two types, the basic award and the compensatory award. In addition, in some cases special awards may be made. Where the employer unreasonably fails to comply with a reinstatement or re-engagement order then the tribunal can award an additional award.

The basic award

- The basic award is equivalent to a redundancy payment, ie:
  - $1\frac{1}{2}$ weeks' pay for each year of service over the age of 41
  - 1 week's pay for each year of service over the age of 22
  - $\frac{1}{2}$ week's pay per year of service at any lower age.
- The statutory limit for a week's pay applies
- Only the best 20 years of service can be counted under this provision
- From the age of 64 the complainant loses 1/12 of this entitlement per year over 64 – this is to allow for the fact that at age 65 there would be no entitlement.

- Those who are dismissed or selected for redundancy for
  - being safety representatives or members of a health and safety committee
  - being employee representatives, or seeking election as such; or
  - being occupational pension scheme trustees

  are entitled to a special minimum basic award – currently £2,700
- The basic award can be reduced:
  - where the employee has unreasonably refused an offer of reinstatement by the employer
  - for the employee's conduct before the dismissal
  - for any redundancy payment made by the employer in respect of the dismissal
  - to ensure that the employee is not doubly compensated where the dismissal also amounts to unlawful discrimination under the sex or race discrimination legislation.

The compensatory award
- The compensatory award is to compensate the complainant for the loss which he has suffered by being unfairly dismissed insofar as that loss is attributable to action taken by the employer.
- The compensatory award is subject to an upper limit – currently £11,300.
- The losses which can be compensated include:
  - any expenses incurred by the employee as a result of his dismissal; and
  - the loss of any benefit which the employee might have expected to have had if it were not for the dismissal, including any redundancy payment in excess of the statutory amount which the employee might otherwise have expected to have.
- Some factors may reduce the compensation which the employee is ultimately awarded:
  - The complainant is under a duty to mitigate the losses arising from the dismissal.
  - The tribunal can reduce the compensatory award, to such degree as it considers just and equitable, where the employee has in any way contributed to his own dismissal.
  - If the employer has given the employee any payment on the grounds that the dismissal was on account of redundancy then the amount by which that payment exceeds the basic award is to be taken to reduce the compensatory award.

Special compensatory award
- Where the complainant is dismissed because of being or carrying out the duties of:
  - a safety representative
  - a member of a safety committee

- a trustee of an occupational pension scheme
- an employee representative (or seeking election as such)

a special compensatory award must be made. This is:
  - 104 weeks' pay, or £13,775, whichever is the greater, subject to an upper limit of £27,500 or
  - where the tribunal has ordered reinstatement or re-engagement and the employer has failed to comply with the order, then, unless it was not practicable to comply with the order, the amount of the special award is increased to 156 weeks' pay or £20,600, whichever is the greater.
  - If the complainant has:
    - prevented the reinstatement or re-engagement order from being complied with or
    - refused an offer by the employer to reinstate him

    then the tribunal can reduce the special award by such amount as it considers just and equitable, having regard to that finding
  - Where the employee is over 64 then the special compensatory award is reduced by 1/12 per month by which the employee's age exceeds 64.
  - The tribunal can reduce the special compensatory award where it considers it just and equitable to do so because of the conduct of the complainant before dismissal.
  - (The special basic award made in such cases is dealt with under the basic award – *above*.)

36.13 Redundancy payments

Previously Part VI EPCA amended by Employment Acts 1982 and 1989 and TURERA. Now ss 136 to 181 ERA.

(a) *General right*
  (i) Dismissal for redundancy
      An employee is dismissed for redundancy if he is dismissed wholly or mainly because the employer:
      - stops running the business for which the employee was employed
      - moves it to a different place; or
      - the requirement for employees to carry out the type of work that the employee can be asked to do ceases or diminishes.
  (ii) Lay off and short-time working as redundancy
      There are complex provisions under which an employee who has been laid off or kept on 'short time' (ie earning less than half his normal weekly wage because of lay off) can give notice to his employer claiming a redundancy payment if that situation continues for four weeks or for six weeks in a thirteen-week period. The employer can give a counter-notice disputing liability to pay a redundancy payment. The most usual case where this will be relevant is where the employer informs the employee

that there is a likelihood of not less than 13 weeks' full employment which will begin within four weeks of the date of the employer's counter-notice. Where such full-time employment is available the employee will not be entitled to a redundancy payment.

(b) *Qualifications for entitlement*
   • The employee must be continuously employed for two years.
   • The employee must either be:
      • below normal retiring age for employees of that type in the business in question; or
      • below 65.
   Where the employee is over 64 he loses 1/12 of his redundancy payment for every month over 64.

(c) *Amount of redundancy payment*
   A redundancy payment is $1\frac{1}{2}$ weeks' pay for each year of employment over the age of 41. One week's pay for every year over the age of 22 and $\frac{1}{2}$ week's pay for any year below 22. The maximum number of years which can be taken into account in calculating a redundancy payment is 20 and the amount of 'a week's pay' is limited by statute.

(d) *Exclusions from entitlement*
   (i) Summary dismissal
      An employee is not entitled to a redundancy payment if he is or could be summarily dismissed unless:
      • the reason for dismissal is that he has taken part in a strike; or
      • he is dismissed during the minimum notice which he is entitled to be given by the employer by statute
      in which case it is for the tribunal to decide what redundancy payment, if any, the employee ought to get.
   (ii) New employment and the trial period
      • If the employee accepts or unreasonably refuses suitable alternative employment then he is not entitled to a redundancy payment.
      • Where, before the employee's employment terminates, he is offered new employment to begin within four weeks of the end of his current employment, then
         • if the terms and conditions of the new contract are different from the old contract the employee has a four-week statutory trial period in which to decide whether or not to continue in the job. If he does not, or if the employer dismisses him for a reason arising out of the new terms and conditions, then he is considered to have been dismissed from the original redundancy date.
         • where the employee needs retraining, then a longer trial period can be agreed in writing between the employer and the employee.

(e) *Claiming a redundancy payment*
   A claim for a redundancy payment must be made within six months of dismissal to a tribunal or to the employer. If a claim is made late, within a year of

the dismissal, then the tribunal can award a redundancy payment if it appears to the tribunal to be just and equitable that the payment should be made. It should be noted that if the employer becomes insolvent or fails to pay the employee a redundancy payment to which he is entitled, a claim may be made directly to the Secretary of State for a redundancy payment to be paid.

36.14 Insolvency

Originally in EPCA as amended by Insolvency Act 1985 and 1986, Bankruptcy (Scotland) Act 1985, Employment Acts 1989 and 1990 and TURERA, now ss 182 to 190 ERA.

These provisions allow for the payment of certain debts owed to an employee by an employer who becomes insolvent to be paid by the Secretary of State.

36.15 Agreements to exclude the protection of the ERA

(a) *Fixed-term contracts*

Where the employee is under a fixed-term contract of one year or more, entitlement to claim unfair dismissal can be excluded.

Where the employee is under a fixed-term contract of two years or more, entitlement to claim a redundancy payment can be excluded.

(b) *Compromise agreements*

Introduced by TURERA.

Generally, the rights under employment legislation, including those under the ERA, cannot be contracted out of. TURERA introduced a new system whereby a valid agreement can be reached to exclude an employee's rights to claim provided that a solicitor or barrister is involved and that certain specific statutory requirements are adhered to. (A settlement of a case can still be validly reached with the assistance of a Conciliation Officer.)

37 Employment Subsidies Act 1978

Allows for payments to be made to employers under schemes to alleviate unemployment. There have been two schemes set up under this Act in Great Britain, the Temporary Employment Subsidy and the Youth Employment Subsidy.

38 Equal Pay Act 1970

Amended by Sex Discrimination Acts 1975 and 1986, Equal Pay (Amendment) Regulations 1983 and Pensions Act 1995. The Industrial Tribunals Rules of Procedure (Amendment) Rules 1996 (SI 1996 No. 1757) amend the procedure used to deal with equal value claims.

38.1 Equality clause

The Act provides that a woman's contract is to have an equality clause implied into it if it does not specifically contain one. The effect of the equality clause is to modify the woman's contractual conditions so that they are no less favourable than those of a man who is engaged on *like work* or on *work rated as equivalent*.

38.2   The Equal Pay (Amendment) Regulations 1983

(a) These provide a new head under which parity may be claimed – where the man is on *work of equal value* to that of the woman. The effect of this amendment is threefold:

    (i)   it has 'opened up a far wider field for claims than existed under the old law. Comparisons can now be made between totally dissimilar jobs, in different pay structures and across different collective bargaining groups'

    (ii)   it allows for an independent expert to evaluate and compare jobs even where the employer has no job evaluation scheme in operation. (The Industrial Tribunals Rules of Procedure (Amendment) Rules 1996 (SI 1996 No. 1757) amended the erstwhile *requirement*, brought in with the 1983 Regulations, that an independent expert must be appointed in equal value cases. The 1996 amendments to the tribunal rules mean that the tribunal can now decide whether or not in the particular case an independent expert should be appointed. One of the difficulties in practice had been the length of time that such cases have been taking due, in part, to the length of time taken to obtain independent experts' reports); and

    (iii)   it allows an existing job evaluation scheme to be scrutinised by the tribunal to ensure that there is no discriminatory bias within the scheme itself.

(b) For *equal value* claims the original *material difference* defence is amended to a *material factor* defence. (This, broadly, allows the employer to justify a difference on non-sex-based grounds – personal differences or market forces.)

(c) The Act and the amendments apply equally to men, who can, therefore, claim equality of terms with a woman on *like work*, *work rated as equivalent*, or on *work of equal value*.

39   European Communities Act 1972 – Treaty of Rome

The European Communities Act 1972 brought into effect the application of certain European regulations to UK law. Certain provisions of the Treaty of Rome are important in employment.

(a) Provisions allowing for free movement of labour across EC borders.

(b) Equal access for EC nationals to social security benefits.

(c) Equal pay. Article 119, which provides for 'equal pay for equal work', is wider than the Equal Pay Act 1970 and has direct effect in the UK.

40   Factories Act 1961

Amended by Sex Discrimination Act 1986 and Employment Act 1989, Manual Handling Operations Regulations 1992 (SI 1992/2793), Provision and Use of Work Equipment Regulations 1992 (SI 1992/2932), Workplace (Health, Safety and Welfare) Regulations 1992 (SI 1992/3004), Personal Protective Equipment at Work Regulations 1992 (SI 1992/2966) and Education Act 1993.

Consolidates previous Factories Acts of 1937, 1948 and 1959, establishes standards of health, safety and welfare in factories. It is intended, eventually, to bring all the health and safety provisions under the ambit of codes and regulations made under the Health and Safety at Work etc. Act 1974. The previous restrictions on the hours of work of women and young persons contained in the Factories Act were lifted by the Employment Act 1989.

41   Family Law Reform Act 1969

Reduced the age of majority from 21 to 18.

42   Finance Acts

The provisions of the Finance Acts, so far as they affect taxation of employment under Schedule 'E', are largely consolidated into the Income and Corporation Taxes Act 1988.

42.1   Finance Act 1989

Amends Income and Corporation Taxes Act 1988.
(a) Allows a tax exemption for those over 60 on payments made by them in respect of private medical insurance
(b) Increases the limits on 'payroll giving' schemes (charitable donations made directly from the payroll which are treated as a tax-free item) from £240 to £480.

42.2   Finance Act 1990

(a) Where an employer provides a 'workplace nursery', this benefit is no longer treated as a taxable benefit.
(b) Employees who use their private car for work may now claim a capital allowance for their car – ie some of the capital value of the car can be written off against the employee's Schedule E tax liability.

42.3   Finance Act 1991

(a) Mortgage interest relief, which could previously be set off against the whole of the employee's tax liability, can now only be set off against basic rate income tax. The maximum mortgage which qualifies for mortgage interest relief remains at £30,000.
(b) Employees who undertake vocational training which they pay for themselves will qualify for income tax relief on the costs of the training from April 1992.
(c) From 1 January 1992 employers who have an 'executive share option scheme' will be allowed to give participants up to 15% discount on share prices provided that the company also operates a general share option scheme for all employees.
(d) From 1 January 1992 an investment of up to £3,000 may be made in a personal equity plan (PEP) in a single company in addition to the £6,000 investment which can be made in a general PEP. This is to encourage employee share ownership.

(e) Where an employer provides the employee with a portable telephone the employee will have to pay tax on it on the basis of a new 'scale rate'.

42.4 Finance Act 1993

Amends Income and Corporation Taxes Act 1988.
(a) Sets out a new method of calculating the notional benefit of a company car and fuel provided for private use for the tax years 1994/1995 onwards.
(b) Allows tax relief on the reasonable removal expenses reimbursed by an employer in respect of an employee moving to take up a new job or in cases where the employer moves or the employee's job is moved.

43 Fire Precautions Act 1971

Amended by the Health and Safety at Work etc. Act 1974 and by the Fire Safety and Safety of Places of Sport Act 1987.

Governs fire precautions in all places of work. The provisions governing fire precautions contained in the Factories Act 1961 and the Offices, Shops and Railway Premises Act 1963 are repealed.

44 Fire Safety and Safety of Places of Sport Act 1987

Amends Fire Precautions Act 1971 and Health and Safety at Work etc. Act 1974.

Tightens up on matters such as means of escape from premises in cases of fire and allows for improvement notices and prohibition notices to be served where an occupier of premises has inadequate provision either for escape in cases of fire, or for fire fighting.

45 Food Safety Act 1990

Gives local authorities powers to oversee company canteens to ensure food safety standards are met.

46 Further and Higher Education Act 1992

Amends Education Act 1944, Chronically Sick and Disabled Persons Act 1970, Sex Discrimination Act 1975, Race Relations Act 1976, Employment Act 1989.

Makes any provision in a contract of employment in the further education sector void insofar as it provides either:
(a) that the employee shall not be dismissed by reason of redundancy; or
(b) that if the employee is dismissed by reason of redundancy he shall receive a larger redundancy payment than would be payable under the ERA.

47 Health and Safety at Work etc. Act 1974

Amended by Sex Discrimination Act 1986, Fire Safety and Safety of Places of Sport Act 1987 and Employment Act 1989.

It is ultimately intended to replace all existing safety legislation with regulations and codes of practice under this Act. To facilitate this transfer of jurisdiction, the

Act absorbs the inspectorates provided for by a multitude of statutes dealing with safety matters (eg Factories Act 1961, Explosives Act 1875, Mines and Quarries Act 1954) into a single Health and Safety Executive which now deals with all such matters.

Part I of the Act has four purposes:

(a) securing the health, safety and welfare of persons at work
(b) protecting other persons against risks to health and safety arising out of, or in connection with, the activities of persons at work
(c) preventing the unlawful acquisition and possession of explosives and other highly flammable and dangerous substances and controlling their use and storage
(d) controlling the emission of noxious substances into the atmosphere.

These purposes are to be achieved to some extent by the Act itself which puts a general duty on employers, employees, the self-employed and other people who are concerned with the premises to have regard for the safety of others and themselves. Sections 15 and 16, respectively, provide for regulations to be made and for codes of practice. It should be noted that breaches of Part I of the Act give rise to criminal liability but not to civil liability, which is, therefore, largely the province of existing statutory and common law duties. Part II of the Act amends and repeals in part the Employment Medical Advisory Services Act 1972. Part III of the Act widens the scope of building regulations made under the Public Health Act 1936. (The Act amends and repeals parts of the Fire Precautions Act 1971, the Employment Medical Advisory Services Act 1972 and the Employment and Training Act 1973.)

48   Health and Safety (Consultation with Employees) Regulations 1996 (SI 1996 No. 1513)

Amends ERA and Safety Representatives and Safety Committees Regulations 1977 (SI 1977/500).

In 1994 the EC Commission successfully brought a case against the UK complaining of the UK's failure to implement the requirement for consultation in relation to collective redundancies and transfers of undertakings in cases where trade unions were not recognised. The HSCE Regulations are a spin-off of this in that the Framework Directive (Directive 89/391/EEC), articles 10 and 11, requires that there be consultation with employees on matters affecting health and safety. Until these regulations were brought in, the requirement for employers to consult with employees was restricted to employments in which trades unions were recognised (*see Safety Representatives and Safety Committees Regulations 1977 (SI 1977/500)*).

48.1   Exclusions

Employment in domestic households is excluded.

Where employees are represented by safety representatives under the Safety

Representatives and Safety Committees Regulations 1977 SI 1977 No. 500 (SRSCR), the employer must consult with those safety representatives. Where there are no safety representatives the employer is required to consult under these regulations (cf. the Collective Redundancies and Transfer of Undertakings (Protection of Employment) (Amendment) Regulations 1995 SI 1995 No. 2587 where the employer has a choice as to whether to consult with a recognised trade union or with employee representatives).

48.2   Representatives of employee safety

Representatives of employee safety are elected by employees specifically to represent them on health and safety matters. They are entitled to paid time off for training, to carry out their functions and to stand for election. They are specifically protected from dismissal and action short of dismissal related to their functions under the ERA (qv).

An employee representative's duties are to make representations to the employer:
(a) on general matters of health and safety and on potential hazards and dangerous occurrences at the workplace which affect, or could affect, the group of employees he represents; and
(b) to represent the group of employees he represents in consultations at the workplace with health and safety inspectors.

48.3   Consultation

(a) *With whom*
  The employer must consult either employees who are affected or representatives of employee safety who have been elected by the group of employees in question to represent them.
(b) *About what*
  The employer must consult in good time on matters regarding employees' health and safety at work, in particular on
  1   the introduction of:
    • measures which may substantially affect employees' health and safety; and
    • new technology
  2   arrangements for:
    • appointing people to be responsible for statutory health and safety duties
    • nominating people to deal with serious and imminent dangers at work and danger areas
  3   health and safety information which he is required to provide by statute
  4   planning of health and safety training he is required to provide by statute.
(c) *Requirement to provide information*
  The employer must provide information for the employees or their representatives to have all relevant information which he has available which will allow

them to participate fully and effectively in consultation. Certain types of confidential information are excluded from this requirement.

49   Health and Safety (Display Screen Equipment) Regulations 1992 (SI 1992 No. 2792)

This is one of the 'Six-pack' Regulations introduced in 1992 arising from European health and safety directives.

(a)   *Display screen users*

The requirements of these regulations are limited to 'display screen users', ie those to whom *all or most* of the following criteria apply:

(i)   the employee requires display screen equipment (DSE) to do the job – other means are not readily available

(ii)   the employee has no discretion as to whether or not to use DSE

(iii)   the employee requires training in use of DSE to do the job

(iv)   the employee normally uses DSE for continuous periods of an hour or more

(v)   the employee uses DSE in this way more or less daily

(vi)   fast transfer of information between the user and the screen is an important requirement of the job

(vii)   performance requirements demand high levels of attention and concentration by the user – eg where the consequences of error may be critical.

(b)   *Work stations for DSE users*

(i)   Work stations used by DSE users must be assessed for risks and reassessed if there has been a significant change. The matters which need to be looked at range from the equipment itself (including the software) and the desk and chair the user will use, to the surroundings in which they will use it – including consideration of matters such as glare and reflection on the screen, ambient noise, heat from equipment, etc.

(ii)   By December 1996 all work stations were required to meet a specification laid down in the schedule to the Display Screen Equipment Regulations.

(c)   *Daily work routine of DSE users*

(i)   The job of DSE users should be so designed as to ensure that they have regular breaks or changes in activity to reduce their workload on the equipment

(ii)   this may be done by:
  •   job design – putting natural breaks into the work itself; or
  •   providing for specific breaks (such breaks should be taken away from the screen where possible).

(d)   *Eye tests*

(i)   Regular professional eye tests must be provided by the employer for DSE users at the employer's expense

(ii)   If there is a specific visual difficulty which may reasonably be considered to be caused by work on DSE the employer must provide a further eye test if the employee so wishes.

    (iii)   The employer must provide spectacles where they are needed specifically for DSE work (but not if the problem with using DSE would be overcome by using spectacles which the person requires for normal use).

(e) *Health and safety training*

    (i)   the employer must ensure that DSE users are trained in health and safety aspects of DSE; and

    (ii)   that DSE users are retrained in health and safety if their work station is modified significantly.

(f) *Health and safety information*

    (i)   Employers must provide DSE users with information on all aspects of health and safety re. DSE work stations.

    (ii)   Employer's must provide DSE users with information on measures taken by him to comply with:

- the requirement to give breaks to DSE users
- the requirement to give health and safety training to DSE users
- the availability of eye testing and specialised spectacles where these are required.

50   Health and Social Security Act 1984 (largely repealed)

Amends Social Security Pensions Act 1975 and Social Security and Housing Benefits Act 1982.

Amended by Social Security Act 1985 and Wages Act 1986, is now largely repealed by the Social Security (Consequential Provisions) Act 1992.

51   Immigration Act 1971

Amends and replaces previous immigration laws. Is amended by the Asylum and Immigration Act 1996.

Generally, except for certain occupations such as dentistry and medicine, any non-patrials require work permits to work in the UK. The provisions of the Act have now been amended to allow EC nationals to take up employment in the UK freely.

52   Income and Corporation Taxes Act 1988

Consolidates much of the earlier legislation concerning taxation of income and other benefits arising from employment.

Amended by Finance Acts 1989 and 1993, Police Act 1997.

53   Industrial Training Act 1964

Repealed by Industrial Training Act 1982 and Agricultural Training Board Act 1982 except for s 16 allowing local education authorities to provide vocational training.

54   Industrial Tribunals Act 1996

Repeals and consolidates various provisions from EPCA, TULRA and TURERA.

Consolidates the legislation dealing with the powers and constitution of industrial tribunals and the Employment Appeals Tribunal (EAT) and with conciliation of tribunal cases.

55 Industrial Tribunals Extension of Jurisdiction (England and Wales) Order 1994 (SI 1994/1623)/(Scotland – SI 1994/1624)

Extends the jurisdiction of industrial tribunals as originally provided for by s 131 EPCA which, as amended by TURERA, is now s 3 Industrial Tribunals Act 1996.

Allows for breach of contract claims to be brought to an industrial tribunal where the claim arises or is in issue on termination of employment.

The limit on such claims is £25,000 and certain claims, such as those involving personal injuries and restraint of trade, are excluded from the tribunal's jurisdiction. A claim under these provisions must be brought within three months of the date of dismissal or within such further time as is reasonably practicable where it is not reasonably practicable to meet the three-month time limit.

56 Industrial Tribunals Rules of Procedure (Amendment) Rules 1996 (SI 1996 No. 1757)

Amends the tribunal rules concerned with equal-value cases to allow a tribunal to consider whether or not they need an independent expert's report when they are considering a case brought under the 'work of equal value' provisions. There are other modifications to the requirements concerning independent experts' reports which are also intended to speed up the progress of equal-value claims.

57 Industrial Training Act 1982

Amended by Employment Act 1989.

Consolidates the law relating to industrial training boards.

58 Industry Act 1975 and 1980

The 1975 Act is amended by the Industry Act 1980.

The 1980 Act removes much of the ambit and effect of the 1975 Act. The National Enterprise Board (NEB) is retained but those parts of the Act dealing with disclosure of information to the government and to trade unions are repealed.

The remaining objectives of the NEB are:
(a) to promote the efficiency and international competitiveness of British industry
(b) to provide and protect productive employment; and
(c) to prevent important firms from coming under unacceptable foreign ownership.

59 Industry Act 1981

Amends the financial limits imposed on the NEB by earlier Acts and gives the Secretary of State for Employment power to make grants or loans to anybody:
(a) to promote the practice of engineering

(b) to encourage and improve links between industry and educational courses; and
(c) to encourage young persons and others to take up careers in industry and to follow appropriate educational courses.

60 Insolvency Act 1985

Amended Employment Protection (Consolidation) Act 1978. This amendment is now consolidated into ERA.

Replaced s 122(4) EPCA with a new subsection setting out certain items which are to be treated as items of arrears of pay for purposes of s 122 (*see also Insolvency Act 1986 below*). These are:
(a) guarantee payment
(b) remuneration from suspension on medical grounds
(c) payment in respect of statutory time-off; and
(d) payment under a protective award.
This is now consolidated into s 184(2) Employment Rights Act 1996.

61 Insolvency Act 1986

Amends Employment Protection (Consolidation) Act 1978.
Certain employee debts are given priority over other debts:
(a) remuneration for up to eight weeks preceding the date when the employer became insolvent up to a statutory maximum
(b) where an employee's employment was terminated before the employer became insolvent, then arrears of holiday pay of up to six weeks can be recouped.

62 Job Release Act 1977

Provides for early retirement for those approaching pension age for purposes of making work available for the unemployed or otherwise for mitigating the effects of high unemployment.

63 Jobseekers Act 1995

Amends the Social Security Contributions and Benefits Act 1992, Social Security Administration Act 1992, Social Security (Incapacity for Work) Act 1994.

This Act was passed to replace Unemployment Benefit with a new Jobseeker's Allowance.

63.1 Statutory exclusions from entitlement

(a) *Trade dispute*
An employee who is unemployed either because he is taking part in a trade dispute or has a direct interest in it is disqualified from entitlement to Jobseeker's Allowance. He will be qualified to receive Jobseeker's Allowance again if, during the trade dispute:
(i) he becomes bona fide employed elsewhere
(ii) his employment is terminated by reason of redundancy; or

(iii) he has bona fide resumed employment with his employer, but has subsequently left for a reason other than the trade dispute.
(b) *Misconduct and voluntary leaving*
An employee can be disqualified from entitlement to Jobseeker's Allowance for up to 26 weeks if he:
- loses his employment through misconduct; or
- voluntarily leaves employment without just cause.

For these purposes a person who is dismissed for redundancy, after having volunteered for redundancy, is not to be considered to have left voluntarily.
(c) *Reduction for pension payments*
The Act provides that regulations can be made to take into account the amount of any personal or occupational pension which an individual is entitled to in determining the amount of Jobseeker's Allowance which is payable. Under the previous law pension payments were taken into account in ascertaining an individual's entitlement to unemployment benefit if that individual was over 55 years old.

64 Local Government Act 1988

Restricts Local Authorities from having regard to 'non-commercial' considerations when awarding public supply or works contracts. Such non-commercial considerations include:
(a) terms and conditions of employment afforded by contractors to their employees
(b) composition of the workforce, and arrangements for promotion, transfer or training of the workforce – ie discrimination consideration

(Whilst considerations of discrimination by a contractor on grounds of *race* may be looked at as a relevant factor by an authority when considering whether or not to award a contract to a contractor, considerations of *sex* discrimination may not be taken into account.)

'Contract compliance' – ie forcing contractors to have non-discriminatory policies and terms and conditions of employment which are as good as the local levels – is, in a general sense, outlawed by this provision.
(c) whether the contractor's workers are employed or self-employed
(d) conduct of contractors or workers in any industrial disputes
(e) any interests a contractor may have in any other country
(f) any political affiliation or activities of the contractor.

65 Local Government and Housing Act 1989

Amended by Disability Discrimination Act 1995.

Prevents senior local authority staff from becoming members of any local authority.

66 Management of Health and Safety at Work Regulations (SI 1992 No. 2051)

This is one of the 'Six-pack' Regulations introduced in 1992 arising from European health and safety directives.

The Regulations amend Safety Representatives and Safety Committees Regulations 1977 (SI 1977 No. 500), Shops and Railway Premises Act 1963 and Factories Act 1961.

(a) *Risk assessment*

   (i)   The Regulations require an employer to make a suitable and sufficient assessment of

- risks to the health and safety of employees at work; and
- risks to the health and safety of others who are affected by the conduct of his undertaking

so that appropriate protective and preventative measures which need to be taken to comply with any statutory provision can be identified. This includes measures which need to be taken under Control of Substances Hazardous to Health Regulations 1988 as well as the more general health and safety requirements under HASWA and the other 'six-pack' directives, etc.

   (ii)   The employer must also identify:

- significant findings of the assessment which is made; and
- any groups of employees assessed as being at special risk

and record these findings in writing.

   (iii)   The risk assessment must be reviewed if:

- there is reason to suspect that it is no longer valid; or
- there has been a significant change in the matters to which it relates.

   (iv)   Where a number of employers share a workplace they must co-operate in fulfilling their statutory health and safety duties. They should also take all reasonable steps to co-ordinate their health and safety efforts and they must provide each other with information about the risks to the other employer's employees arising from their operations.

(b) *Health and safety arrangements*

   (i)   The Regulations require employers to make and put into effect appropriate arrangements, having regard to the nature of their activities and the size of the undertaking, for the effective planning, organisation, control, monitoring and review of the preventive and protective measures shown by the risk assessment to be necessary. This requirement is aimed at having some sort of system for the ongoing monitoring and review of health and safety measures in the workplace.

   (ii)   Where the employer employs more than five people these arrangements must also be recorded in writing.

(c) *Health surveillance*

Employers are required to ensure that employees are provided with such health surveillance as is appropriate having regard to the risks to their health and safety which are identified by the risk assessment which has been carried out. If a particular type of operation could potentially have an adverse effect on an employee's health, then the employer must assess the employee's health on an ongoing basis.

The type of health surveillance which would apply in the majority of employments is exemplified by providing eyesight tests for those using VDUs.

(d) *Health and safety assistance*

   (i)   Employers must appoint one or more competent persons to assist in undertaking the measures they need to take to comply with the various statutory health and safety provisions. Where more than one person is appointed the employer must ensure that they all co-operate with each other.

   (ii) The employer is required to consult with the appropriate people or the appropriate body about the appointment of his assistant under this provision. The appropriate people or bodies are:

   - where a trade union is recognised, safety representatives under Safety Representatives and Safety Committees Regulations 1977 (SI 1977 No. 500)
   - where no trade union is recognised, then either the employees themselves or representatives of employee safety appointed under Health and Safety (Consultation with Employees) Regulations 1996 (SI 1996 No. 1513).

(e) *Procedures for serious and imminent danger and for danger areas*

   (i)   Employers need to establish and where necessary give effect to appropriate procedures to be followed in the event of serious and imminent danger to employees. This includes procedures for:

   - making sure that those who are exposed to serious and imminent danger are informed:
     - of the nature of the hazard; and
     - the steps taken or to be taken to protect them from it
   - enabling people to stop work and go to a safe place in the event of serious, imminent and unavoidable danger
   - preventing people from returning to work whilst a serious and imminent danger continues.

   (ii) Employers must nominate sufficient competent people to implement any evacuation procedures. Safety representatives, employees or representatives of employee safety must be consulted about these nominations (as per (d)(ii) above). The most obvious situation to which this applies is evacuation in the case of fire or bomb threat.

   (iii) Employers must also ensure that no employee has access to an area to which access is restricted on health and safety grounds unless that employee has received adequate health and safety training.

(f) *Information for employees*

Employers must give employees comprehensible and relevant information on:
- risks to their health and safety identified by the risk assessment
- preventative and protective measures taken following the assessment
- the procedures to be followed by the employees in cases of serious and imminent danger – in most cases this will entail having at least a set fire evacuation procedure
- any risks to employees arising out of the operations of another employer who shares premises with the employer.

(g) *Employees' duties and training*

  (i)   Employers must take into account an employee's capabilities to do a task, in health and safety terms, before entrusting that task to that employee.

  (ii)   Employers must also ensure that employees are provided with adequate health and safety training during working hours:
- when they are recruited
- when they are exposed to new or increased risks because of:
  - a transfer or change of responsibility
  - the introduction of a new system of work, new machinery or new technology
  - a change in the system of work or in the way in which existing machinery is used.

  (iii) Employees must use any health and safety equipment provided to them by their employer, including machinery, materials and safety equipment, in accordance with any training and instruction given by the employer

  (iv) Employees must inform their employer or a fellow employee with health and safety responsibility of any situation or matter which affects them or their work:
- which they reasonably consider to be a serious and imminent danger to health and safety; or
- which they reasonably consider to be a shortcoming in the employer's arrangements for health and safety protection.

This duty on an employee is limited to what his training and experience would make him realise was a serious risk or a shortcoming in health and safety arrangements.

67 Manual Handling Operations Regulations 1992 (SI 1992 No. 2793)

This is one of the 'Six-pack' Regulations introduced in 1992 arising from European health and safety directives.

The Regulations amend Shops and Railway Premises Act 1963 and Factories Act 1961.

(a) Manual handling is concerned with moving objects around usually by lifting, but also by pushing or pulling.

(b) Manual handling which shows in the general risk assessment as potentially involving risk of injury should be avoided if possible.

(c) If manual handling cannot be avoided, it should be automated as far as is practicable.

(d) Where it is not possible to avoid manual handling, an assessment must be made of all manual handling which is necessary and which involves a risk of injury. The assessment needs to be repeated if it gets out of date.

(e) Steps must be taken to reduce the risk to employees to the lowest possible level including:
  • increasing automation
  • reducing weights to be carried
  • putting the weights into smaller packages
  • making the packages more manageable
  • redesigning the workplace or the job where the lifting is carried out to minimise risks.

(f) Employers must also provide guidance on:
  • lifting techniques
  • the weight of each load; and
  • where the centre of gravity of a load is not central, on which side the load is heaviest.

68   Oil and Gas (Enterprise) Act 1982

The Oil and Gas (Enterprise) Act 1982 contains provisions repealing the extensions of the sex and race discrimination legislation contained in the Employment (Continental Shelf) Act 1978. An Order will need to be made under the 1982 Act to give effect to these repeals.

69   Offices, Shops and Railway Premises Act 1963

Amended by Fire Precautions Act 1971, Health and Safety at Work etc. Act 1974, Manual Handling Operations Regulations 1992 (SI 1992/2793), Provision and Use of Work Equipment Regulations 1992 (SI 1992/2932) and Workplace (Health, Safety and Welfare) Regulations 1992 (SI 1992/3004), Police Act 1997.

The purpose of this Act was to establish a code of safety and welfare for those places of work not covered by the then existing legislation. It is concerned largely with welfare provisions such as adequate ventilation, light, warmth and washing facilities (much of which is now covered by Regulations). Fire precautions in premises subject to this statute are now covered by the 1971 Act as amended.

70   Patents Act 1977

Amended by Copyright, Design and Patents Act 1988.

Provides a method of determining the ownership, as between employer and employee, of an employee's inventions and also provides for the employee to be given compensation for his invention in certain circumstances. The invention will belong to the employer if:

(a) it was made in the course of either the employee's normal duties or special duties which had been assigned to him; and in either case an invention was, in the circumstances, to be reasonably expected from his carrying out these duties; or
(b) the employee made the invention in the course of his duties and because of the nature of his duties and the particular responsibilities arising from the nature of those duties he was under a special obligation to further his employer's interests. In all other cases the invention belongs to the employee.

An application for compensation for an invention may be made to the Comptroller or Patents Court if:
(i)	the invention belongs to the employer under the Act; and it has been patented; and it is of outstanding benefit to the employer; or
(ii)	where the patented invention belongs to the employee and has been assigned to the employer or the employer has been granted an exclusive licence to the invention by the employee; and the benefit derived by the employee is inadequate in relation to the benefit derived from the patent by the employer.

The amount of compensation, in either case, is to be a 'fair share' of the benefit which the employer has derived from the patent.

71   Payment of Wages Act 1960 (repealed)

Repealed by Wages Act 1986.

72   Pensions Act 1995

Amends the Equal Pay Act 1970, Sex Discrimination Act 1975, EPCA, Companies Acts 1985 and 1989, Insolvency Act 1986, Social Security Act 1989, SSBCA, Pensions Schemes Act 1993, and various other Acts in connection with the equalisation of State pension age.

Is amended by the ERA

72.1   General regulation of occupational pension schemes

(a) The Act sets up a closer regulatory system to ensure the security of employees' pensions. It introduces the Occupational Pensions Regulatory Authority which has power to remove trustees of a pension scheme or to suspend them. The OPRA can also appoint trustees to replace any it removes. The OPRA's powers extend to winding up a pension scheme if it considers that that is necessary to protect the interests of the generality of the members of the scheme.
(b) There are restrictions on employer-related investments and on employers taking the benefit of any surplus in the scheme, as well as minimum funding requirements for 'final salary' schemes. A provision, waiting to be brought into effect by statutory Order will make it an offence for an employer not to pay over to the pension scheme any pension contributions deducted from employees.
(c) The OPRA's inspectors are given powers to enter onto premises for purposes

of investigating whether the regulatory provisions applicable to an occupational pension scheme have been complied with. The powers are in much the same terms as the powers which social security inspectors are given in relation to social security inspections under the Social Security Administration Act 1992 *(see below)*.

(d) A minimum number of trustees are required to be nominated by members of the Scheme and the Act requires an independent trustee to be appointed in certain circumstances. There are also provisions for employee trustees to be appointed.

(e) A statutory Order may be made bringing into effect provisions under which trustees will be required to increase the value of pensions under the scheme by the rise in the cost of living index or 5 per cent (whichever is the lower). This will not apply to any part of the pension stemming from additional voluntary contributions.

(f) The Act introduces the Pensions Compensation Board which can make compensation payments to the Trustees of a trust scheme if the employer is insolvent and if the value of the assets of the scheme has been reduced unlawfully to a level of 90 per cent or less of the liabilities of the Scheme.

(g) The powers of the Pension Ombudsman are prospectively extended by the Act.

72.2 Employee trustees

The provisions for paid time off and training for employee pension scheme trustees are now contained in the ERA (qv).

72.3 Equalisation of state pensionable age

State pensionable age is increased for women born after 6 April 1950. There is a gradual increase, over a ten-year period, so that pension age will ultimately be equalised at 65 for all those born after 6 April 1955.

72.4 Equal treatment in relation to occupational pension schemes

Provision for equal treatment in relation to occupational pension schemes was originally introduced by Schedule 5 Social Security Act 1989. These provisions were enacted to give effect to EC Directive 86/378/EEC on the equal treatment for men and women in relation to occupational social security schemes. Following the ECJ's judgment in Barber v Guardian Royal Exchange Assurance Group [1990] IRLR 240 it became clear that equal treatment under occupational pension schemes from 17 May 1990, the date of the ECJ's judgment in Barber, had to be treated as a matter of equal pay. The provisions of this Act, therefore, overtook the provisions of the Social Security Act 1989, as far as pensions were concerned. The Act adopts a framework for equal treatment in relation to occupational pension schemes which closely mirrors the provisions of the Equal Pay Act 1970. These provisions are applicable to pensionable service on or after 17 May 1990.

(a) *The equal treatment rule*
  - The equal treatment rule relates to the terms on which people become members of the scheme and to the terms on which members of pension schemes are treated. This includes:
    - *Discretionary matters*: Trustees or managers of pension schemes are often given discretionary powers under the scheme. The Act provides that where there is any discretionary power, which could be exercised in a way which is detrimental to a woman, then the effect of the equal treatment rule is to bar the trustees from exercising their discretion in that way.
    - *Dependants' benefits*: Where the scheme provides benefits for dependants of members (for example, life assurance cover or survivor's pensions) then these too are subject to the requirement of equal treatment between scheme members.
  - All occupational pension schemes which do not specifically contain an equal treatment rule are deemed to include one. Where the rules of the scheme do not allow for the scheme to be altered to accommodate the requirements of an equal treatment rule, the trustees are given the power to alter the scheme by resolution to accommodate the equal treatment rule and its effects. Any such alteration can be retrospective.
(b) *Who can claim?*
  - Those who are on 'like work', 'work rated as equivalent' or engaged on 'work of equal value' to:
    - a comparator of the opposite sex; or
    - a comparator of the opposite sex and of the same marital status (where benefits differ with marital status)

    are entitled to have any term of the scheme, which is unfavourable to them, modified so as to be as favourable to them as it is to their comparator.
(c) *Exclusions*
  - *Material difference*: As with equal pay there is an exclusion where the trustees of the scheme can show that the difference in the terms or effects of the scheme are due to a material difference between the two employees other than the difference in their sex.
  - *Maternity and family leave*: The equal treatment rule for pensions is subject to the equality provisions, in the Social Security Act 1989, relating to maternity and family leave.
  - *State pension*: A difference in treatment is allowed, in pension schemes, if that difference arises purely out of the difference in entitlement to a State retirement pension between the sexes.
  - *Actuarial calculations*: A difference in treatment is allowed if it is the result of a difference in actuarial calculations for each sex in respect of:
    - the level of the employer's contributions to the scheme; or
    - the level of benefit from the scheme.

(d) *Claims*
- The equal treatment rule is treated as one with the requirement for equal treatment in relation to pay under the Equal Pay Act 1970 and a case may be brought to an industrial tribunal in the same way.
- To be entitled to claim, the employee must bring a claim within six months of the time when he or she was employed in a category of job to which the pension scheme in question applied.
- The Sex Discrimination Act 1975 is amended to include, within the definition of grounds on which it is unlawful to victimise an employee, the fact that a person has made a claim under these provisions.

73 Pension Schemes Act 1993

Amends the Social Security Act 1973, Social Security Pensions Act 1975, EPCA, Social Security Act 1979, Social Security Act 1980, Social Security Act 1981, Social Security and Housing Benefits Act 1982, Health and Social Security Act 1984, Insolvency Act 1985, Insolvency Act 1986, Social Security Act 1986, Social Security Act 1988, Social Security Act 1989, Employment Act 1989, Social Security Act 1990, TULRA, Social Security Act 1993.

Amended by the Pensions Act 1995.

This Act was passed to consolidate and amend some of the law relating to pension schemes.

73.1 'Contracted-out pension schemes'

The Act contains the definition of 'contracted-out employment' for pension purposes. Contracted-out pension schemes are those which are contracted out of the earnings-related part of the State scheme. To be contracted out pension schemes need to meet the appropriate requirements of the Act.

73.2 Reclaiming unpaid pension deductions

The Act deals with the case where an employer becomes insolvent, in a case where an employee has had deductions made from pay for pension scheme contributions. In such cases if any such contributions have not been paid to the pension scheme, someone acting on behalf of a pension scheme can apply to the Secretary of State for payments to be made equivalent to any such sums. If the Secretary of State fails to pay then a person acting for the pension scheme can apply to an industrial tribunal to order those payments to be made. Outstanding contributions to an employer's pension scheme are given priority in the event of the employer's bankruptcy to the extent that those contributions relate to the 12 months prior to insolvency.

73.3 Individuals' rights in respect of pension schemes

(a) *Preservation of rights under pension schemes – short-term employees*
    (i)   A 'short-term' member of a pension scheme is one who has had at least

two years' pensionable service in an employment with a contracted-out
pension scheme. Short-term employees must be provided with a preserved pension unless the accrued pension is transferred to another
scheme.

(ii)   The rules of the scheme must not contain any rules which will or could
result in a disparity of treatment of a short-term pension scheme member
as compared with the way in which a long-term member would be treated
in the same circumstances.

(iii) Short-term members who have a preserved pension in a pension scheme
must have their pensions increased to the same extent as those who
remain in the scheme.

(b) *Choice of schemes*

The Act allows employees to opt for personal pension schemes rather than the
employer's pension scheme and makes void any contractual provision which
purports to make membership of the employer's occupational pension scheme
mandatory.

(c) *Voluntary contributions*

Strict limitations are imposed on a scheme's ability to restrict a member's entitlement to make additional contributions to the scheme.

(d) *Disclosure of information*

The Secretary of State is empowered to make Regulations to require that certain categories of people are entitled to be given information about pension
schemes. (Several sets of Regulations have been made under these provisions.)

- The people who are entitled to this information are:
  - members and, in the case of an occupational pension scheme, prospective
    members
  - spouses of the above
  - those to whom the scheme is applicable or prospectively applicable; and
  - in the case of an occupational pension scheme an independent trade union
    which is recognised to any degree for collective bargaining purposes.
- The above categories of people can be required, by Regulations, to be kept
  informed of:
  - the constitution of the scheme
  - the scheme's administration and finances
  - the rights and obligations that arise or may arise under the scheme
  - any other matters which appear to the Secretary of State to be relevant
    either to:
    - occupational or personal pension schemes in general; or
    - to schemes of a description to which the scheme in question be-
      longs.
- The Regulations can specify when the required information is to be given as
  a matter of course and where it need only be given on application.
- Where a person, who is entitled to any such information is not given it then

they must serve a default notice on the trustees. If they still do not get the information within a further 14 days then they can apply to the county court for an Order that the information be provided.

(e) *Pensions Ombudsman*

The Act establishes a Pensions Ombudsman who can deal with disagreements between a member of a pension scheme (or his dependants) and the trustees or managers of the scheme. The Ombudsman is empowered to deal with problems of all types, whether they are matters of fact, of law or of alleged maladministration. The Pensions Ombudsman's powers are amended by the Pensions Act 1995.

74 Personal Protective Equipment at Work Regulations 1992 (SI 1992 No. 2966)

This is one of the 'Six-pack' Regulations introduced in 1992 arising from European health and safety directives. The Regulations amend the Factories Act 1961.

(a) Personal protective equipment (PPE) is industrial body armour. Because it is cumbersome and uncomfortable for the wearer the Regulations, as a whole, encourage PPE to be used only in the last resort where other forms of protection cannot be used or are inadequate. Where PPE is used a risk assessment must first be carried out to ensure that the PPE proposed is suitable and it is obviously important that all the PPE supplied to an employee is mutually compatible.

(b) Where PPE is provided it must be maintained in an efficient and clean state and in good repair. Proper accommodation must also be made available for its storage.

(c) The employee must be given training on the use and purpose of the PPE and on keeping it in a proper condition and must report any defect in, or loss of, the PPE to his employer. Both the employer and the employee are under a duty to ensure that the PPE is used properly.

(d) The Regulations contain several pages of guidance to help employers to select appropriate PPE for their particular needs.

75 Police Act 1997

Amends Offices Shops and Railway Premises Act 1963, Employers' Liability (Compulsory Insurance) Act 1969, Employers' Liability (Defective Equipment) Act 1969, Employment Agencies Act 1973, Sex Discrimination Act 1975, Race Relations Act 1976, Income and Corporation Taxes Act 1988, ERA.

The provisions of the Police Act 1997 which are relevant for employment purposes are a new system whereby Certificates of Criminal Records can be issued. It is intended that the Certificates under these provisions will be issued by a separate body set up specifically for this purpose. No date has been set for this legislation to take effect. (The legislation was passed by the last Conservative Government shortly before the 1997 General Election.)

(a) *Criminal Conviction Certificate*
  (i)   Under the new legislation anyone can apply to the Secretary of State for a Criminal Conviction Certificate provided that:
        • the application is made on a prescribed form and
        • the appropriate fee is paid.
  (ii) A Criminal Conviction Certificate gives details of any criminal convictions the person may have, other than any spent convictions (*for 'Spent convictions' see Rehabilitation of Offenders Act 1975*).

(b) *Criminal Record Certificate*
  (i)   Where a person is being considered for employment, or is seeking to join a profession, which is exempted from the provisions of the Rehabilitation of Offenders Act 1975 (ie one where questions regarding spent convictions – 'exempted questions' – must be answered fully and truthfully by the applicant), then a Criminal Record Certificate (CRC) can be obtained.
  (ii) An application for a CRC must be:
        • made in the prescribed form
        • accompanied by the appropriate fee
        • countersigned by a 'registered person'. (A person or body can be registered on application to the Secretary of State if the person or body is likely to ask exempted questions.) The registered person must also certify that the CRC is required for purposes of an exempt question.
  (iii) A CRC will give details of:
        • any convictions – whether or not spent; and
        • any cautions.
  (iv) A copy of the CRC is sent to the registered person who signed the application.

(c) *Enhanced Criminal Record Certificate*
  (i)   Where an Applicant is applying for certain types of employment or licence (*see (ii) below*) an Enhanced Criminal Record Certificate (ECRC) can be sought.
  (ii) The form and method of application is much the same as for a normal CRC (*see above*) but, for an ECRC to be issued, the 'exempted question' must be being asked
        • in the course of considéring the applicant for a position whether paid or unpaid which either:
          • involves regularly caring for, training, supervising or being in sole charge of persons aged under 18; or
          • is of a kind specified in Regulations made by the Secretary of State which involves regularly caring for, training, supervising or being in sole charge of persons aged 18 or over
        • for a purpose relating to any of the following:
          • gaming licence application
          • lotteries and lotteries management licence application

- registration as a child minder
- placing children with foster parents.

(iii) An ECRC will give details of:
- all relevant information relating to the applicant which is recorded in central records; and
- the Secretary of State must also ask all Chief Police Officers in any relevant force to provide any and all information which in that Officer's opinion:
  - might be relevant to the employment or other application which has given rise to the exempt question being asked and which ought to be included in the certificate; and
  - all such information which ought not to be included in the certificate in the interests of the prevention of crime but which can be disclosed to a registered person (in a separate document to the ECRC) without harming the interests of the prevention of crime.

(iv) A copy of the ECRC and any accompanying document is sent to the registered person who signed the application.

(d) *Accuracy*
  (i) Where an applicant believes that a CCC, CRC or ECRC is inaccurate he can apply to the Secretary of State in writing for a new certificate. Where the Secretary of State is satisfied that the certificate is inaccurate a new certificate must be given.
  (ii) The Secretary of State may require that an applicant for a certificate under these provisions has fingerprints taken to establish that person's identity. Any Regulations made under this provision may make provision for the destruction of the fingerprints in certain specified circumstances.

(e) *Unlawful disclosure*
  (i) A member, officer or employee of a registered body may only disclose information from a certificate to:
  - a fellow member, officer or employee of the registered body in the course of his duties
  - to a member, officer or employee of the body which asked the registered person to obtain the information for them.

  Any breach of this is a criminal offence.
  (ii) There are further provisions which make it a criminal offence for a person or body on whose behalf the information has been obtained to further disclose such information or for a person to whom any such information is disclosed to divulge it to anyone else.

76 Provision of Work Equipment Regulations (SI 1992 No. 2932)

This is one of the 'Six-pack' Regulations introduced in 1992 arising from European health and safety directives. The Regulations amend Shops and Railway Premises Act 1963 and Factories Act 1961.

The primary requirements imposed by these Regulations are beyond the scope of this work in that they concern the suitability of machinery and work equipment for the job and the environment in which they are used. They require work equipment to conform to European standards and to have appropriate controls. Such matters will generally be taken into account in the purchase and installation of the work equipment. There are, however, some aspects of these Regulations which may affect employees at a more day-to-day level.

(a) *Maintenance and repair*
   (i)   There is a duty to ensure that all work equipment is properly maintained and repaired.
   (ii) A maintenance log needs to be kept for each machine.

(b) *Use, repair and modification of dangerous machinery*
   Where the use of a machine is likely to involve risks to health and safety
   (i)   only people who are properly trained may use the equipment (adequate training for use of the machine is also required); and
   (ii) such equipment must only be repaired or modified by those who are properly trained.
         This means that employers need to make sure that machine operators who are not properly trained do not make their own informal modifications or try to repair such machines.

(c) *Health and safety information*
   Any person who uses, or who supervises the use of, work equipment must have adequate health and safety information and where appropriate readily comprehensible written instructions about the use of the equipment. This must include instructions on:
   (i)   the conditions in which, and methods by which, the equipment may be used
   (ii) any foreseeable abnormal situations – and action to be taken if such a situation occurs
   (iii) any conclusions drawn from experience in using the particular equipment.

(d) *Guarding equipment and employees*
   (i)   There is a requirement properly to guard machinery and to exclude people from the danger areas surrounding the equipment.
   (ii) It is important to ensure that maintenance can be carried out safely – if at all possible with the machine switched off.
   (iii) There is a requirement to protect employees against anything coming off or out of any piece of work equipment and giving rise to injury; this includes protection against bits flying off, fire, discharge of any particle, dust or gas, etc.
   (iv) Employees must be protected against very high or low temperatures generated by parts of the machine.

(e) *Working conditions*
   (i)   The stability of the machine when in use must be ensured. This is particularly important in the case of portable machinery.

(ii) The suitability and sufficiency of the lighting for the work which is carried out with the machine must also be ensured.

77 Race Relations Act 1976

Repeals and replaces the Race Relations Acts 1965 and 1968.

Amended by Employment Act 1989, Further and Higher Education Act 1992, Education Act 1993 and Race Relations (Remedies) Act 1994, Police Act 1997.

77.1 Grounds on which discrimination is unlawful

Makes discrimination unlawful on the grounds of colour, race, nationality or ethnic or national origin in employment and other fields. It is unlawful to discriminate against a person either directly or indirectly on these grounds.

77.2 Genuine occupational qualifications

Exceptions are made where race, etc. is a genuine occupational qualification for a particular job.

77.3 The Commission for Racial Equality

The Act establishes the Commission for Racial Equality (CRE) whose duties are:
(a) to work towards the elimination of racial discrimination; and
(b) to promote equality of opportunity and good relations between persons of different racial groups generally; and
(c) to monitor the working of the Act and to make recommendations to the Secretary of State to amend the Act if and when necessary.

The CRE is given wide powers of investigation and power to draw up codes of practice to eliminate discrimination in employment (*see below*). An employee or applicant for a job who has been discriminated against may be awarded compensation by an industrial tribunal. The address of the CRE is:

Elliot House
10–12 Allington Street
London SWIE SEH
Tel. 0171–828–7022

CRE Code of Practice 1984

In April 1984 the CRE Code of Practice for the elimination of racial discrimination and the promotion of equality of opportunity in employment came into force. As with similar codes it is not legally binding but its provisions, and questions of whether or not an employer has complied with those provisions, are admissible in evidence before an industrial tribunal. The Code's two most important recommendations on the responsibilities of employers concern:
1. The implementation of equal opportunity programmes and
2. The monitoring of such programmes with the aid of analysis of the ethnic origins of the workforce and of job applicants.

Specifically, the Code recommends that:

(a) employers should adopt, implement and monitor an equal opportunity policy
(b) the policy should be clearly communicated to all employees
(c) overall responsibility for the policy should be allocated to a member of senior management
(d) where appropriate, the policy should be discussed and agreed with trade unions or employee representatives
(e) training and guidance should be provided for supervisory staff and other relevant decision-makers to ensure they understand their position in law and under company policy
(f) employers should monitor the effects of selection decisions and of personnel practices/procedures to assess whether equal opportunity is being achieved. The information needed for effective monitoring may be obtained in a number of ways but, says the Code, will best be achieved by records showing the ethnic origins of existing employees and job applicants. (Abstracted from *IPM Digest*, No. 229, August 1984, pp. 9–10.)

78   Race Relations (Remedies) Act 1994

Amends the Race Relations Act 1976.

This Act was passed following the decision that the maximum limit on compensation fixed by the Sex Discrimination Act 1975, at that time £11,000, did not meet with the UK's obligation under European law to provide an adequate remedy in cases of sex discrimination. The upper limit of compensation in sex discrimination cases was removed by the Sex Discrimination and Equal Pay (Remedies) Regulations 1993 (SI 1993/2798) with effect from November 1993. The Race Relations (Remedies) Act 1994 abolished the upper limit on compensation for race discrimination with effect from 3 July 1994 by repealing s 56(2) of the RRA; thus bringing the remedies for sex and race discrimination back into line with each other.

79   Rehabilitation of Offenders Act 1974

Provides that a conviction, other than one involving a sentence of more than 30 months' imprisonment, may become rehabilitated if the offender commits no further serious offences during the rehabilitation period. The rehabilitation periods vary with the sentences imposed and the age of the offender is also taken into account. Where a conviction has expired, under the terms of the Act, it is unlawful for the offender to be refused employment or to be dismissed from employment on the grounds of that conviction. Certain professions and occupations are excluded from the provisions of the Act; these include the legal profession, accountants and teachers.

80 Reserve Forces Act 1980

Amended by Reserve Forces (Safeguard of Employment) Act 1985 and greatly amended and replaced by the Reserve Forces Act 1996.

Amends Trade Union and Labour Relations Act 1974, Employment Protection (Consolidation) Act 1978.

The provision for reserve forces and Territorial Army to be called up are now contained in Part VI Reserve Forces Act 1996. They were previously made under s 10 of the 1980 Act. Orders authorising the calling out of reserve forces/TA are made by the Queen, under the hand of the Secretary of State, under s 10 of the Act.

In the Gulf War such an order was made to protect the employment of reservists who volunteered for service with the forces as well as those who were called up (*see also Reserve Forces (Safeguard of Employment) Act 1985 below*).

81 Reserve Forces Act 1996

Amends Reserve Forces (Safeguard of Employment) Act 1985.

Repeals and replaces much of the Reserve Forces Act 1980 and the whole of the Reserve Forces Act 1982.

81.1 Definition

Reserve Forces are: the Royal Fleet Reserve, Royal Naval Reserve, Royal Marine Reserve, Army Reserve, Territorial Army, Air Force Reserve and the Royal Auxiliary Air Force.

81.2 Calling up reserve forces

(a) The statutory provisions allowing for reserve forces to be called up are now contained in Part VI Reserve Forces Act 1996.

(b) Reserve forces may be called up
  - where the nation appears to be in imminent danger
  - where a great emergency has arisen or there is an actual or apprehended attack on the UK
  - where war-like operations are in preparation or progress
  - where the Secretary of State considers it desirable to use armed forces for:
    - the protection of life or property outside the United Kingdom; or
    - in operations anywhere in the world to save lives or property in time of disaster or apprehended disaster.

(c) In cases where an Order calling out reserve forces is made, the employment of those who are called up is protected under the Reserve Forces (Safeguard of Employment) Act 1985. In the Gulf War an order was made calling up reservists who had volunteered for service with the forces as well as those who were actually called up. This had the effect of ensuring that the employment of volunteers was protected under Reserve Forces (Safeguard of Employment) Act 1985.

81.3   Special agreements/Employee agreements

(a) Special agreements:

An employee who is employed to work for more than 14 hours per week may, with the consent of his employer, enter into an agreement which will make him liable:

- to be called out for permanent service anywhere in the world; and
- to fulfil any training obligations specified in the agreement

for a period of up to nine months.

(b) Employee agreements:

    (i)   Employee agreements are agreements primarily between the employer and Secretary of State for employees to enter into agreements to become special members of the reserve forces.

    (ii)   An employee can enter into an agreement to become a special member of the reserve forces in such circumstances with his employer's consent.

(c) A person who is called up under either of these schemes can seek a deferral or exemption from call up.

(d) Employees who are called up under these schemes have their employment protected under the Reserve Forces (Safeguard of Employment) Act 1985.

81.4   Former members of the forces

(a) Former members of the regular forces are liable to be recalled unless they are 55 or over, or if they were discharged or transferred to the reserve forces 18 or more years previously. (Former members of the Royal Navy or Royal Marines only remain liable to be recalled for six years after discharge or transfer to the Reserves.)

(b) Employees who are recalled under these provisions have their employment protected under the Reserve Forces (Safeguard of Employment) Act 1985.

82   Reserve Forces (Safeguard of Employment) Act 1985

Amends Reserve Forces Act 1980, Employment Protection (Consolidation) Act 1978, Tribunals and Enquiries Act 1971.

Repeals National Service Act 1948, Reinstatement in Civil Employment Act 1950.

Amended by Reserve Forces Act 1996.

(a) *When is protection given?*

The Act provides safeguards, in relation to employment, for: reservists and those who have entered into special or employee agreements who are called up into full-time service in the forces and those who are recalled to full-time service in the forces.

(NB Those who volunteer for service without being called up are generally outside this statutory protection, but in the Gulf War an Order was made calling up volunteers so that their employment would be protected – *see Reserve Forces Act 1996 above.*)

(b) *The rights provided for by the Act*

(i)   Right to return

The Act provides for an employee who was employed within four weeks before being called up to be offered a job by his last employer, at the first reasonable opportunity after his release from full-time service, and to be kept in that job for no less than the minimum statutory period.

(ii)   Minimum statutory period

The minimum statutory periods for which the employee must be employed after returning from the forces depends on the employee's length of service before being called up.

If the employee had less than 13 or more than 26 or 52 weeks' employment before call-up he will be entitled to be kept on for at least 13, 26 or 52 weeks respectively, following his reinstatement. The only restriction on this right is that it must be reasonable and practicable for the employer to keep the employee on (or to keep him on on the terms and conditions on which he was reinstated) throughout that period.

(iii) Right to return to what?

The employee's right is primarily a right to be offered employment in the occupation in which he was engaged before his full-time service with the forces began, on terms and conditions no less favourable than those which would have applied if he had not been away. If it is not reasonable and practicable for the employee to be taken back into his former occupation on those terms and conditions, then he is entitled to be offered a job in the most favourable occupation and on the most favourable terms and conditions which are reasonable and practicable in his case.

(iv)   Right to return when?

The employee must be offered employment to begin at the first opportunity (if any) at which it is reasonable and practicable for it to begin, after the date which he has notified to the employer as the date on which he will be available for work (*see (c) below*).

The right to be offered a job is also limited to the first six months after the ex-employee's service with the forces ends. After this the former employer has no duty to take the employee back (unless he is required to take the employee back following any order to that effect made by a Reinstatement Committee).

(v)   Effect of refusing employer's offer

Once the employer has offered the employee a job his obligation to 'take the employee back' is *prima facie* discharged. However it will not be discharged if the applicant believes that he has reasonable cause for not taking the job which is offered and he, or someone acting on his behalf, notifies the employer in writing of his reasons for not taking the job 'as soon as may be' after the job is offered.

(c) *Enforcement of these statutory rights*

Either the applicant, or someone acting on the applicant's behalf, must apply in writing to the applicant's former employer asking that the applicant be taken back into employment. The application must be made within the first two weeks after the applicant's release from full-time service with the forces. If the applicant is sick or if because of some other reasonable cause the applicant cannot apply within the prescribed time, the application will still be valid provided it is made as soon as it reasonably can be.

The applicant must also provide his former employer with a date when he will be available to take up work if it is offered. That date must be within 21 days of the latest date on which the application can be validly made (this is, again, extended where the applicant is sick or where it is otherwise reasonable for him not to comply).

An application to be taken back into employment ceases to have effect 13 weeks after it was made, unless it has been renewed during the 13-week period. It is also preserved during any period whilst there are any proceedings pending regarding the application.

An applicant can apply to a Reinstatement Committee if he considers that any of his rights under the Act (including his right to be taken back and to be kept on for the minimum statutory period) are being or have been denied to him.

(d) *Statutory presumptions as to whether or not it is reasonable and practicable to take an employee back*
The Act provides that the fact that taking the applicant back will involve dismissing someone else does not, of itself, make taking the applicant back either unreasonable or impracticable. The only exception to this is where taking the employee back would involve dismissing another employee who had been employed for longer than the applicant by the date when the applicant left employment to join the forces. Where both the applicant and the other employee were called up then the comparison is between the length of service given by each before the first of them left to join the forces.

(e) *Continuity of employment*
Employees who are entitled to apply to be employed by their former employer, and who are taken back within six months of the termination of their full-time service with the forces, have their employment before they were called up treated as continuous with their employment after their return to work. The actual period of absence does not itself count as a period of continuous employment.

83 Safety Representatives and Safety Committees Regulations 1977 (SI 1977 No. 500)

The Regulations were amended by the Management of Health and Safety at Work Regulations 1992 SI 1992/2051 and by Health and Safety (Consultation with Employees) Regulations 1996 (SI 1996 No. 1513).

These Regulations were made under the Health and Safety at Work etc. Act 1974 and provide for consultation where trade unions are recognised. Where trade unions are not recognised employers are required to consult either the employees themselves or representatives of employee safety, under the Health and Safety (Consultation with Employees) Regulations 1996 (SI 1996 No. 1513) (qv).

(a) *Appointment of safety representatives*

    (i)   Where an independent trade union is recognised by an employer then the union can appoint safety representatives. The union must inform the employer in writing who they have appointed.

    (ii)   Employees appointed as safety representatives should normally have had two years in that employment or in similar employment so that they have experience of the type of workplace.

(b) *Functions of safety representatives*

    (i)   The employer must consult with safety representatives

- with a view to establishing and maintaining arrangements for effective co-operation between the employer and his employees to ensure the health and safety at work of employees and
- checking the effectiveness of those arrangements
- on the introduction of:
  - any measures which may substantially affect employees' health and safety; and
  - new technology
- arrangements for:
  - appointing people to be responsible for statutory health and safety duties
  - nominating people to deal with serious and imminent dangers at work and danger areas
- health and safety information which he is required by statute to provide
- planning of health and safety training he is required by statute to provide

    (ii)   To carry out inspections of the workplace

- once every three months after giving written notice to the employer; or
- more often:
  - with the employer's consent
  - where there has been a substantial change in the conditions of work, such as the introduction of new machinery, since the last inspection
  - where relevant advice from the Health and Safety Executive (HSE) has been given since the last inspection
  - where there has been a notifiable accident or dangerous occurrence or where a notifiable disease has been contracted. In such cases safety representatives may inspect the area affected and any other areas which it is necessary to inspect to determine the cause.
- The employer may accompany the safety representative on any such inspection.

    (iii) To investigate

- potential hazards at the workplace

- dangerous occurrences at the workplace
- causes of accidents at the workplace
- complaints by employees relating to their health and safety at work.

(iv) To make representations to the employer:
- arising out of the above investigations and
- on general matters affecting the health, safety and welfare of the employees at the workplace.

(v) To represent employees in consultations with the Health and Safety inspectorate.

(vi) To attend Safety Committee meetings as a safety representative.

(c) *Requirement to provide information and documentation*

(i) The employer must provide information for safety representatives so that they have all the relevant information that the employer has available which will allow them to carry out their duties. Certain types of confidential information are excluded from this requirement.

(ii) The employer must allow safety representatives to inspect and take copies of all health and safety documentation which the employer is obliged by statute to keep – other than documentation relating to an identifiable individual.

(d) *Facilities*

(i) Safety representatives are entitled to paid time off:
- to carry out their duties as safety representatives; and
- to undergo training.

(ii) If a safety representative is refused paid time off he can complain to an industrial tribunal within three months of the time off being refused (or where that is not reasonably practicable within such further time as is reasonably practicable).

(iii) The employer must provide safety representatives with such facilities and assistance as they may reasonably require to carry out their duties.

(e) *Safety committees*

(i) An employer must establish a safety committee where two or more safety representatives request him to do so in writing.

(ii) Where safety representatives request the establishment of a safety committee the employer must:
- consult with those representatives and trade union representatives in the areas which will be covered by the safety committee
- post a notice, giving the composition of the safety committee, where all relevant employees will be able to see it; and
- establish the safety committee within three months' of the request being made.

84   Sex Discrimination Act 1975

Amended by Employment Act 1989, Further and Higher Education Act 1992 and Education Act 1993 and Sex Discrimination and Equal Pay (Remedies) Regulations 1993 (SI 1993/2798), Pensions Act 1995, Police Act 1997.

Makes discrimination on grounds of sex or marital status unlawful. Its provisions are similar in extent and effect to those of the Race Relations Act 1976. The main differences are:

(a) the Sex Discrimination Act (SDA) does not cover discrimination in pay – this is dealt with by the Equal Pay Act 1970 as amended.

(b) the SDA makes special provision to deal with discrimination in matters relating to death or retirement (amended by SDA 1986, Employment Act 1989 and prospectively by the Pensions Act 1995 – *see commentary under Sex Discrimination Act 1986*). The SDA excludes special, more beneficial, provisions relating to pregnancy from being treated as discrimination.

(c) the Equal Opportunities Commission (EOC) is established by the Act and has an equivalent function to the Commission for Racial Equality (CRE) in matters related to sex discrimination, including the power to draw up codes of practice (*see below*). The EOC also has jurisdiction to monitor and review the working of the Equal Pay Act 1970.

85   Sex Discrimination Act 1986

Amended by Employment Act 1989 and ERA its provisions are also amended by the Pensions Act 1995.

Amends Sex Discrimination Act 1975, Employment Protection (Consolidation) Act 1978, Equal Pay Act 1970, Employment Protection Act 1975, Hours of Work Convention Act 1936, Factories Act 1961, Health and Safety at Work etc. Act 1974.

85.1   Employment in private households

The Act removes the right to discriminate, on grounds of sex, where employment is for a private household, except in a case where the amount of intimate contact with a person living in the home or the knowledge of intimate details of a person's life which the employee might come upon means that the householder might reasonably object to having a man/woman do that work.

85.2   Death and retirement

The exclusion of matters related to 'death or retirement' from the sex discrimination legislation under the 1975 Act is largely removed. Whereas in the normal case it is unlawful for an employer to discriminate by dismissing an employee or subjecting her to any other detriment, in cases where the discrimination is concerned with retirement it is unlawful to discriminate by 'dismissing or subjecting [the individual] to any detriment which results in her dismissal or consists in or involves her demotion'. This still allows some scope for discrimination in relation to pension matters. There is an equivalent provision inserted into the Equal Pay Act

1970. The provisions regarding discrimination in relation to pensions are, however, prospectively modified by the Pensions Act 1995 to allow for unequal treatment of men and women in a pension scheme where that treatment would not offend against the 'equal treatment' requirements under the Pension Act 1995.

85.3   Normal retirement age
The 1986 Act amended the exclusion, from claiming unfair dismissal, for those over normal retirement age or statutory pension age so that an employee's claim is only excluded if he has reached either:
(a) 'normal retirement age' for a person holding that position in the organisation (provided that that retirement age is the same for both men and women); or
(b) in any other case, 65.
This provision is now contained in s 109 ERA.

85.4   Terms in collective agreements
The Act invalidates any terms in collective agreements, in an employer's rule and in the rules of qualifying bodies, which are unlawfully discriminatory or which give rise to unlawful discrimination.

85.5   Women's hours of work
The erstwhile restrictions on women's hours of work, under various statutes, are removed.
The address of the EOC is:

Overseas House
Quay Street
Manchester M3 3HN
Tel. 0161–833 9244

86   Sex Discrimination and Equal Pay (Remedies) Regulations 1993 (SI 1993/2798)
Amends the Sex Discrimination Act 1975.
These regulations were passed following the decision that the maximum limit on compensation fixed by the Sex Discrimination Act 1975, at that time £11,000, did not meet with the UK's obligation under European law to provide an adequate remedy in cases of sex discrimination. These regulations remove the upper limit of compensation in sex discrimination cases by repealing s 65(2) Sex Discrimination Act 1975. They came into operation with effect from 22 November 1993.

EOC Code of Practice 1985
The EOC launched its Code of Practice for the elimination of discrimination on grounds of sex or marital status in employment on 30 April 1985. The Code is divided into two main parts. The first deals with the role of good employment practices in eliminating sex and marriage discrimination and the second with the role

of good employment practices in promoting equality of opportunity. The Code does not carry the force of law but both parts will be taken into account by industrial tribunals in proceedings under the Sex Discrimination Acts. As with the CRE Code of Practice which has been in force since April 1984, one of the key recommendations is the formulation and implementation of an equal opportunities policy which, says the EOC, 'will ensure the effective use of human resources in the best interests of both the organisation and its employees'. In summary, the Code's main suggestions for successfully implementing an equal opportunities policy are:

1. The policy must be seen to have the active support of top management.
2. The policy should be clearly stated and, where appropriate, should be included in a collective agreement.
3. Overall responsibility for implementing the policy should rest with senior management.
4. The policy should be made known to all employees and, where reasonably practicable, to all job applicants.
5. Trade unions have an important part to play in implementing genuine equality of opportunity and will obviously be involved in the review of established procedures to ensure they are consistent with the law.
6. The policy should be monitored regularly to ensure that it is working in practice.
7. In a small firm it may be quite adequate to assess the distribution and payment of employees from personal knowledge.
8. In a large, complex organisation a more formal analysis will be necessary, for example, by sex, grade and payment in each unit. This may need to be introduced by stages as resources permit.
9. Sensible monitoring will show, for example, whether members of one sex:
   (a) do not apply for employment or promotion, or that fewer apply than might be expected
   (b) are not recruited, promoted or selected for training development or are appointed/selected in a significantly lower proportion than their rate of application
   (c) are concentrated in certain jobs, sections or departments.

Other aspects covered by the Code include job advertising, selection methods – with particular reference to the avoidance of certain discriminatory questions at interviews – promotion, transfer and training, terms of employment, grievance and disciplinary procedures and victimisation. (Abstracted from the *IPM Digest*, No. 238, May 1985, pp. 1–2.)

87 Sex Disqualification (Removal) Act 1919

Provides that no person shall by reason of sex or marriage be excluded from any public function, any judicial or civil office or post 'or from entering or assuming or carrying on any civil profession or vocation, or for the admission of any incorporated society (whether incorporated by Royal Charter or otherwise) ...'.

88   Shops Acts 1950–1965

Amended by Employment Act 1989 and Deregulation and Contracting Out Act 1994, the relevant provisions of the latter were consolidated into the ERA.

Designed to ensure that shop assistants do not have to work excessive hours and that they are allowed adequate rest periods. (*See also Offices, Shops and Railway Premises Act 1963.*) Certain restrictions on shop workers working on Sundays were removed by the Deregulation and Contracting Out Act 1994, the relevant provisions of which have been consolidated into Employment Rights Act 1996.

89   Social Security Acts 1975, (No. 2) 1980, 1985, 1986, 1988 and 1990 and the Social Security Pensions Act 1975 and the Social Security and Housing Benefits Act 1982 (repealed/ consolidated)

These Acts have been largely repealed and consolidated into the Social Security (Contributions and Benefits) Act 1992 and the Pension Schemes Act 1993.

90   Social Security Act 1989

Amended by Employment Act 1990, Social Security Act 1990, Pension Schemes Act 1993 and Pensions Act 1995.

Amends Social Security Acts 1986 and 1988.

Section 23 and Schedule 5 of the Act were enacted to give effect to EC Directive 86/378/EEC on equal treatment for men and women in relation to occupational social security schemes. The main area in which these provisions were intended to operate was in relation to pension schemes. But this changed dramatically following the ECJ's judgment in Barber v Guardian Royal Exchange Assurance Group [1990] IRLR 240 and a number of later cases, which further explained the European equal treatment requirements in relation to pension schemes. Equal treatment under occupational pension schemes from 17 May 1990, the date of the ECJ's judgment in Barber, had to be treated as a matter of equal pay which meant that it had to be dealt with rather more stringently than was envisaged by the 1989 provisions. The provisions of this Act, insofar as they relate to pension schemes, were, therefore, overtaken by the Pensions Act 1995. The only areas in which the 1989 provisions have been brought into effect are unfair maternity and family leave provisions. It should be borne in mind that these are social security measures and, as such, apply to social security as well as employment benefits.

(a) *Entitlement to equal treatment*
- A woman during a period of paid maternity leave and a person during a period of paid family leave (ie a period throughout which the employee is on leave for family reasons) are entitled not to be treated less favourably in relation to any employment-related benefit schemes than they would be if they were at work. This means that:
  - any continuing rights they may have under the scheme must be equivalent to those which would have applied if they had not been on leave; and

- where their overall entitlement under a scheme takes into account a period of maternity or family leave, they must again be in an equivalent position to that which would have applied if they had not been on leave.
- Schemes are, however, specifically permitted to provide more favourable treatment for women who are on maternity leave.
- Where the employee pays into the scheme then the amount that they are required to pay during their maternity leave or family leave must be based on the amount which they are actually being paid during that period.
- Where these requirements are not complied with, and less favourable treatment is given to a woman on maternity leave or to a person on family leave, then they can claim entitlement to the more beneficial treatment afforded to other equivalent members of the scheme:
  - In the case of a woman on maternity leave her treatment must be no less favourable than other women members of the scheme.
  - In the case of those on family leave they are to be treated no less favourably than they would be if they were working normally but only being paid what they are actually paid during their family leave.

(b) *Schemes to which the requirements apply*
  - These requirements apply to any of the following types of scheme which are employment related and which provide different levels of benefit dependent on service. They apply even if the scheme is a discretionary one provided only that the benefits under the scheme are payable in money or in money's worth. Relevant schemes are those providing benefit in respect of:
    - termination of service
    - retirement, old age or death
    - time off because of sickness or invalidity
    - accidents, injuries or diseases connected with employment
    - unemployment; or
    - expenses incurred in connection with children or other dependants; and
    - in the case of an employee include any such benefits which are payable as a result of that person's employment.
  - The following types of scheme are, however, excluded from these provisions:
    - any personal scheme for employees to which the employer does not contribute
    - any insurance scheme which is for the benefit of employees and to which the employer is not a party.

91   Social Security Administration Act 1992

Amended by Statutory Sick Pay Act 1994 and Jobseekers Act 1995.

Together with the Social Security Contributions and Benefits Act 1992, consolidated most social security law. The SSCBA dealing with the substantive law and the SSAA dealing with the administrative parts.

91.1 Investigation, inspection and disclosure of documents

These provisions were originally in the Social Security Act 1986. The Act provides for the appointment of inspectors who are given certain powers.

(a) *Power to enter premises*

An inspector has power under this provision to enter premises where he has reasonable grounds for supposing:

(i)   that there are people employed; or

(ii) that any type of employment agency or 'employment business' is being carried on; or

(iii) that an occupational health scheme is being run or administrated from those premises.

Private dwellings which are not used for business purposes by the occupier (or with his permission) are excluded from this provision.

If required to do so the inspector must produce a certificate of his appointment when seeking to enter any premises.

(b) *Extent of powers*

An inspector's powers extend to:

(i)   entering premises liable to inspection at all reasonable times

(ii) making such examination and enquiry as may be necessary for estimating whether the provisions of the various benefits acts are being complied with

(iii) making such examination and enquiry as may be necessary for investigating any circumstances giving rise to any industrial injuries benefit claim

(iv) examining anyone whom he reasonably believes might be liable to pay Social Security contributions of any sort

(v)   requiring the production of information in accordance with (c) below.

(c) *Disclosure of information to an inspector*

During an inspection those asked are required to provide the inspector with all the information and documentation he may reasonably require, for purposes either:

(i)   of ascertaining whether or not any Social Security contributions are payable in respect of any person and, if they are, whether or not those contributions have been duly paid; or

(ii) whether benefit under any of the benefits acts is or was payable in respect of any person. (This is a potentially far-reaching provision which provides a facility for ensuring that the employees are not also receiving jobseekers' allowance or other undeclared social security benefits.)

In practice, requests for disclosure of information are usually made by post.

91.2 Employer's and employee's notification requirements in respect of SSP and SMP

(a) This Act now contains the requirements for employees to provide their employers with proper medical information of
- any time off for sickness; and
- the expected date of confinement in maternity cases.

(b) The Act also requires employers, if requested to do so by an employee, to provide a statement specifying any days within a period in the case of SSP (or of any weeks within a period, in the case of SMP):
  (i)   in which he considers he is liable to pay the employee SSP or SMP
  (ii) the reason why he does not consider he is liable to pay the employee SSP or SMP for the other days/weeks in that period; and
  (iii) the amount of SSP/SMP which the employer considers himself liable to pay in respect of each of the days or weeks in question.

92 Social Security (Consequential Amendments) Act 1992

This Act is used to repeal the various provisions which needed to be repealed as a consequence of the two social security consolidating statutes: the Social Security Contributions and Benefits Act 1992 and the Social Security Administration Act 1992.

93 Social Security Contributions and Benefits Act 1992 (SSCBA)

Amended by Statutory Sick Pay Act 1994, Social Security (Incapacity for Work) Act 1994 and Jobseekers Act 1995.

Together with the Social Security Administration Act 1992, this Act consolidated a great deal of social security law, the SSCBA dealing with the substantive law and the SSAA dealing with the administrative parts. Most important for employment purposes is the consolidation of the law relating to SSP and SMP.

93.1 Statutory Sick Pay (SSP)

(a) *The benefit*
  (i)   Statutory Sick Pay (SSP) is payable by the employer to an employee for any day of incapacity for work in respect of which the employee meets the statutory qualifications.
  (ii) SSP is a flat-rate benefit. The rate which applies from 6 April 1997 is £55.70p per week. An employee's maximum entitlement in any one Period of Entitlement (see (c) (iii) below) is 28 times the weekly SSP rate.
  (iii) SSP is subject to income tax and national insurance.
  (iv) Daily rate for payment where the employee is entitled for part weeks is:

$$\frac{\text{SSP weekly rate x number of Q days for which payment is due}}{\text{Agreed number of Q days per week}}$$

(v)   Any contractual sick pay goes towards discharging the employer's liability to pay SSP and vice versa.

(vi)   Employers were originally able to recoup the costs of SSP. This facility has now been removed except in very restricted cases – for the current position see Statutory Sick Pay Act 1994.

(vii) Any agreement between an employer and employee for the employer not to pay the employee the SSP to which he is entitled is void. This does not, however, prevent an employer from making deductions from SSP to the same extent as could be made from the employee's normal pay. So where there is a pre-existing arrangement, for example, where deductions are being made in respect of the repayment of a loan, those deductions can continue to be made from any SSP which would otherwise be payable.

(b) *Who is covered?*

(i)   All employees over 16 and who are employed in Great Britain and who pay Class 1 National Insurance contributions (including married women and widows who pay at a lower rate).

(ii)   Part-timers are included provided their earnings are above the Lower Earnings Limit for NI contributions.

(iii) Those with two jobs can claim from both employers.

(c) *Qualification for entitlement*

There are four qualifications for entitlement.

(i)   The day must be a day of incapacity for work.
   - A 'day of incapacity for work' means a day when the employee is, because of a disease or physical or mental disablement, incapable of doing work which he could reasonably be expected to do under his contract of employment.
   - Under the Statutory Sick Pay (General) Regulations 1982 SI 1982 No. 894 an employee who is sick at the beginning of the day or during the working day is deemed to be incapable of work for the whole day if he does no work during that day.

(ii)   The day in question must form part of the Period of Incapacity for Work (PIW).
   - A PIW is a period of four or more consecutive days during which the employee is incapable of work due to sickness.
   - For purposes of a PIW all days of incapacity for work count – regardless of whether or not the employee would normally be working on that day. This also applies to days of incapacity for work which occur before the contract begins and after it ends.
   - Any two PIWs which are separated by not more than eight weeks form a single PIW. This means that the employee will not have to be without SSP during the 'waiting days' which would otherwise apply to the later, linked, PIW (*for 'waiting days', see below*).

(iii) The day must be part of the Period of Entitlement (PE).

- A PE begins at the beginning of the PIW and ends when:
  - the employee's PIW ends
  - the employee's entitlement to SSP from that employer is exhausted
  - his employment has ended; or
  - a pregnant employee reaches the 'disqualifying period' (ie 18 weeks beginning with the 11th week before the expected week of confinement).
- a PE does not arise where at the date when a PE would otherwise begin:
  - the employee is over the age of 65 (the age was increased from 60 for women by the Statutory Sick Pay Act 1994)
  - the employee is under a fixed-term contract of three months or less (unless the employee has actually been employed for more than three months – either under the contract in question, or under one or more contracts each separated by eight weeks or less)
  - the employee is earning less than the lower earnings limit for NI contributions
  - during the 57 days prior to the day in question the employee had at least one day where s/he was entitled to:
    – incapacity benefit
    – maternity allowance; or
    – severe disablement allowance
  - the employee has done no work under his contract of employment (NB Where the employee was employed by the same employer less than eight weeks before the start date of the contract in question, the two contracts are treated as one.)
  - on the day in question there is a trade dispute at the employee's place of work unless the employee can show that he had no interest in that dispute at any time either on or before the day in question
  - the employee is or has been pregnant and the day falls within the disqualifying period unless her pregnancy ended (otherwise than by confinement) before the disqualifying period began.

Where an employee in an excluded category is off sick for four or more consecutive days the employer must complete and send to the employee an exclusion form within 11 days of the employee's first day off sick.

(iv) The day must be a qualifying day (Q day).
  - Q days are those days which, subject to Regulations, the employer and the employee have agreed as being either:
    - the days on which the employee would normally be required to work under his contract; or
    - days which are chosen to reflect the employee's normal working pattern.

- The agreement as to Q days is left largely to the employer and employee but:
  - there must be at least one Q day per week
  - the Q days can vary from week to week
  - Q days must be specified
  - if no Q days are agreed then Q days will normally be those days on which the employee would be required to work. Alternatively, if these cannot be agreed, Q days will be those days which are not specifically agreed to be rest days.

  NB A restriction on the ability of employers and employees to agree Q days was introduced by the Statutory Sick (General) Amendment Regulations 1985 (SI 1985 No. 126). This prevents 'maximising' SSP by setting Q days as being those days when the employee is off sick.
- The employee is not entitled to be paid for the first three Q days in any PIW – these are known as 'waiting days'.

(v)   The absence is duly notified and certified.
- The notification requirements are left to the employer but:
  - he cannot require notification before the first Q day
  - he cannot require notification by a specific time of day (ie notification can only be insisted on by the end of the first Q day)
  - the employer must specify whether notification should be oral or written or both (if written and posted it is the day of posting which is the day of notification)
  - the employer cannot demand notification by the employee in person
  - the employer cannot demand notification in the form of medical evidence of sickness or on a printed form
  - the employer cannot demand notification more than once every seven days during a PE.
- Where notification is late then the employer has discretion to treat the days before notification is given as not being Q days (ie he can withhold SSP and treat the first three Q days after notification as waiting days).
- The Act requires that the employer must obtain suitable evidence of incapacity. This will usually take the form of medical certificates. (*See also Social Security (Medical Evidence, Claims and Payments) Amendment Regulations 1982 – 95 below.*)

93.2   Statutory Maternity Pay (SMP)

The Statutory Maternity Pay provisions came into effect for women whose expected date of confinement was after 21 June 1987. They were brought in by the Social Security Act 1986. The following outline of the Statutory Maternity Pay scheme deals with the provisions of both the Act and various Regulations made under the Act.

(a) *Qualifications for SMP*

To qualify for entitlement to SMP a woman must (subject to very limited exceptions which are not dealt with here) fulfil all of the following requirements:

(i)   She must be over the age of 16.

(ii)   She must be employed under a contract of employment (ie be an employee rather than self-employed).

(iii) She must have completed not less than 26 weeks' continuous service by some time during the 15th week before the Expected Week of Confinement (EWC).

It is noteworthy that the woman need only work during the 15th week before the EWC – she need not work out the whole of that week. (A 'week' for SMP purposes starts from midnight on Saturday night.)

(iv)   She must have had normal weekly earnings which were not lower than the Lower Earnings Limit for NI contributions for the eight weeks of employment ending with the 15th week before the EWC (NB *Normal weekly earnings* are the employee's average earnings over this eight-week period. This means that she would not necessarily have to earn more than the Lower Earnings Limit in each of these weeks.)

(v)   She must have given her employer notice at least 21 days in advance of her absence, stating that she is going to be absent from work wholly or partly because of pregnancy or confinement. This notice must be given in writing if the employer so requests. (NB If the woman also intends to return to work – and has a statutory right to return – after extended maternity leave then she will have to give written notice both of the fact that she is leaving to go on maternity leave and that she intends to return to work. A woman who is entitled only to the statutory minimum of 14 weeks' maternity leave need not give notice of her intention to return.)

(vi)   She must provide her employer with evidence of her EWC (or, if she is receiving SMP because she has already been confined, of her actual week of confinement) by the end of the third week of the Maternity Pay Period (MPP). If there is a good reason stopping her from producing evidence within this time limit, then the evidence can be submitted at any time up until the end of the 13th week of the MPP.

(b) *The Maternity Pay Period (MPP)*

SMP is not payable before the 11th week before the EWC unless the woman has been confined earlier, in which case it is paid in the week following confinement. It is paid on the employee's normal pay days or, if there are no 'normal pay days', on the last day of the month.

The MPP is a flexible period which starts not earlier than the 11th week before EWC nor later than the 6th week before EWC. It lasts for 18 weeks. The MPP may start at any time up to the 6th week before EWC if the woman continues in employment up to the end of the 7th week before EWC, without affecting her overall 18-week entitlement.

If she continues to work beyond the end of the 7th week before EWC then she will lose one week of SMP for each week during which works (she will lose SMP at the lower rate before she loses any of her higher-rate entitlement). No SMP can be paid later than the 11th week after EWC.

(c) *Rates of SMP*

   (i)   There are *two* rates of SMP, the Lower Rate and the Higher Rate:

- *Higher-rate SMP* is 9/10 of the woman's 'normal weekly earnings' for the last eight weeks into the Qualifying Week. Higher rate SMP is payable for the first six weeks of the Maternity Pay Period. Prior to 1994, higher-rate SMP was only payable to women who had completed two years' service by the 11th week before the EWC. The additional service requirement was removed by the Maternity Allowance and Statutory Maternity Pay Regulations 1994 (SI 1994 No. 1230).
- *Lower-rate SMP* is fixed by the Secretary of State for Employment. Once a woman's entitlement to higher-rate SMP is exhausted, the balance of her SMP entitlement is paid at the lower rate.

   (ii)   Originally, as with SSP, the whole of the employer's liability to pay SMP could be reclaimed from the State. Now employers can reclaim:

- in the case of a small employer (ie one whose total annual primary and secondary NI contributions do not exceed £20,000) all SMP plus an additional 5.5% towards the cost of his NI contributions on the payments (see Statutory Maternity Pay (Compensation of Employers) and Miscellaneous Amendment Regulations 1994 (SI 1994 No. 1882))
- in the case of any other employer 92% of the cost of any SMP paid.

   (iii)   The amount of SMP which is reclaimable is reclaimed by deduction from the NI and income tax payments which would otherwise be payable for the period.

(e) *Normal weekly earnings*

A woman's normal weekly earnings are used for two purposes:

First to calculate whether or not her earnings are above the NI Lower Earnings Level (and hence whether or not she is entitled to receive SMP at all).

Secondly, to calculate the woman's Higher-rate SMP entitlement. Normal weekly earnings are calculated as the woman's average weekly earnings over the eight weeks immediately preceding the 14th week before EWC.

Where a woman is paid monthly then her normal weekly earnings for this period are calculated as the sums that she has been paid in the relevant eight-week period divided by the number of months in respect of which she has been paid during that period multiplied by 12/52.

There is also a special definition of 'earnings' for SMP purposes. 'Earnings' are a woman's gross earnings and include any remuneration or profit derived from a woman's employment. Specifically, 'earnings' are taken to include and to exclude the following main items:

Inclusions:
- SSP, contractual sick pay (except for any amount which the woman has contributed towards her own sick pay) and any contractual payment made because of pregnancy or confinement
- Certain sums paid under industrial tribunal orders relating to unfair dismissal and redundancy claims
- Where a woman is paid an annual bonus or some other such lump sum during the relevant eight-week period then this will generally form part of her 'earnings' for that period and a payment of this type may greatly enhance her normal weekly earnings for SMP purposes.

Exclusions:
- Any holiday pay where it is paid from a fund contributed to by more than one employer
- Any payment in respect of a gratuity or offering which is not made by the employer
- Any payment in kind or provision of board, lodgings or other services
- Any pension payment
- Any payment towards expenses incurred by a woman in travelling to her place of employment or training under the Disabled Persons (Employment) Act 1944
- A payment by way of, or derived from, shares apportioned under a statutorily approved profit-sharing scheme
- Any VAT paid on goods or services supplied by the woman
- Any redundancy payment
- Any payment of, or contribution to, expenses incurred by the woman in carrying out her employment (where an 'allowance' is paid in respect of expenses then, if part of that allowance represents a profit in the woman's hands, that profit will be a part of her 'earnings').

(f) *Who is liable to pay?*

A woman's *employer* is liable to pay SMP, provided the woman meets all the conditions. An *employer*, for these purposes, is a person who is liable to pay Secondary Class 1 NI contributions in respect of the woman.

A woman cannot be asked to contribute to her own SMP except that SMP may be set off against any contractual maternity pay which is paid to her. Neither can any agreement be made to modify or exclude any terms of the SMP scheme. There is also provision for any employer, who has dismissed an employee solely or mainly to avoid SMP liability, to be made liable to pay the woman's SMP.

(g) *Exclusion and disqualification from SMP entitlement*

It should be noted that, unlike SSP, which deals with payments and disqualifications in units of 'days', SMP is dealt with in units of 'weeks'. A woman may lose her entitlement to SMP, or to a part of it, in any of the following circumstances:

(i) Working during the MPP
SMP is not payable for any week during which the employee works for
her employer under a contract of employment.

   If the woman works for another employer after her confinement during
her MPP she ceases to be entitled to SMP for the remainder of the MPP.
The woman is obliged to notify her 'liable' employer of any such employment within seven days of its starting. (Since most women are unlikely to
know that they are under a duty to inform you if they work for someone
else during the MPP, your Staff Handbook should make this clear.)

(ii) In legal custody
There is no liability to pay SMP for any week during which a woman is in
legal custody or sentenced to a term of imprisonment (unless the sentence is suspended).

(iii) Death
If the woman dies during the MPP the employer's liability ends in the
week following the week of her death.

(h) *The nature of SMP*
SMP, like SSP, is subject to income tax and NI deductions. There is also a right
to make deductions from SMP in the same way and to the same extent as such
deductions could be made from the woman's ordinary pay.

(i) *Records*
Employers must retain the following records for three years following the tax
year in which the MPP ends:

(i) first notified day of absence in the MPP and the first day of the MPP if
different (eg because of early confinement)

(ii) the weeks of the tax year in which SMP was paid and the amount paid in
each week

(iii) any week in the tax year during an employee's MPP for which no payment was made to her, together with the reason why no payment was
made

(iv) any medical evidence provided to the employer of the EWC or of the
actual week of confinement. If the employer has returned this evidence to
the woman, for her to make any social security claims, it is sufficient if he
keeps a copy. If the medical evidence is of the actual week of confinement
then the employer must keep a note of this. If the employee gives her
employer the birth certificate then this must be returned to her.

(j) *Disputes*
Disputes about SMP liability are generally dealt with through the social security
scheme rather than at industrial tribunal, although the inclusion of SMP in the
definition of 'wages' under the protection of wages provisions of the ERA means
that an employer's failure to pay could be treated as an unlawful deduction and
thus be amenable to litigation before an industrial tribunal. If the employer fails
to pay the woman, or fails to pay the correct amount, or fails to pay it at the right
time, then he can be prosecuted under the social security legislation.

(k) *Special cases*

There are special rules which deal with cases where the employer has dismissed the employee to avoid SMP liability. In such cases the employee may, nonetheless, be able to claim SMP from him provided that she has been continuously employed for at least eight weeks.

If the woman is confined before the 14th week before EWC, she will be entitled to SMP, if she would otherwise have qualified for SMP. The position as it would otherwise have been at the 14th week before EWC may be difficult to judge, however, since the MAT-B 1, which specifies EWC, is not usually available until the 14th week before EWC.

93.3 Industrial injuries

(a) *Entitlement*

- An employee who is injured by an accident arising out of and in the course of his employment will be entitled to industrial injuries benefit.
- Where an accident occurs in the course of employment then there is a presumption that the accident also arose out of that employment unless the contrary is proven.
- An injury caused by an accident to an employee who is, with the employer's permission, travelling to or from work as a passenger in a vehicle provided by or under an arrangement with his employer, is taken to be an industrial injury.
- An injury caused by an accident to an employee in an emergency or supposed emergency, while the employee is on any premises where he is employed to work, is taken to be an industrial injury if he is trying to help people or save property.
- An injury to an employee which was not caused or contributed to by the employee's own misconduct is treated as an industrial injury if it:
  - arises out of another person's misconduct, skylarking or negligence
  - arises out of any steps taken in consequence of another person's misconduct, skylarking or negligence
  - arises out of the behaviour or presence of an animal (including a bird, fish or insect)
  - is caused by or consists of an employee being struck by an object or lightning.
- Employees who suffer from prescribed industrial diseases or prescribed personal injuries (which are not caused by accidents arising out of and in the course of their employment) can also claim industrial injuries benefit.

(b) *The benefit*

Industrial injuries benefit consists of:

(i)   Disablement benefit

- Where the loss of mental or physical faculties arising out of the disablement is not less than 14 per cent (20 per cent where the claim was

made before 1 October 1986) then the employee will be entitled to a disablement pension. In assessing the employee's disability level any pre-existing disability is taken into account as adding to the overall percentage of disability.
  • A higher disability pension is payable where the level of disability is 100 per cent and constant attendance is needed.
(ii) Reduced earnings allowance
A reduced earnings allowance can be claimed in respect of an accident which happened before 1 October 1990 and which resulted in the employee being permanently disabled from following his normal occupation. Where the accident results in a diminution in the employee's earning capacity a reduced earnings allowance may be available to supplement the employee's earnings.
(iii) Retirement allowance
Where a person who was entitled to a reduced earnings allowance retires then they may also be entitled to a retirement allowance which will top-up their normal pension to take into account their reduced earning capacity.
(iv) Industrial death benefit
Provides for a widow's benefit where a person dies who was entitled, or who but for their death would have been entitled, to claim in respect of an industrial injury.

93.4 Notional strike pay

Where an employee is on strike or has an interest in a trade dispute, a set amount of notional strike pay is to be taken into account in assessing any entitlement he may have to social security benefits. This notional sum is taken into account in assessing the employee's entitlement to benefit whether or not he actually receives it.

94 Social Security (Incapacity for Work) Act 1994

Amends the Social Security Contributions and Benefits Act 1992 (SSCBA) and the Social Security Administration Act 1992.

The major thrust of this Act is to bring in a new way of assessing a person's ability or inability to work. This method of assessment is only relevant for benefits under the SSCBA itself and even then is expressly not applicable to assessment of inability for industrial injuries or SSP purposes. From an employment point of view it therefore has very little effect. Other, employment-related provisions in the Act amend existing legislation and are dealt with in the relevant statutes.

95 Social Security (Medical Evidence, Claims and Payments) Amendment Regulations 1982

These regulations provide that medical practitioners need not give national health insurance certificates to cover the first seven calendar days when a person is ill.

96 Statutory Sick Pay Act 1991 (repealed)

Amends Social Security and Housing Benefits Act 1982 and Social Security Acts 1985 and 1986.

Repealed and consolidated into the Social Security Contributions and Benefits Act 1992 and the Social Security Administration Act 1992.

97 Statutory Sick Pay Act 1994

Amends the Social Security Contributions and Benefits Act 1992 and the Social Security Administration Act 1992.

(a) *Removal of right to recoup SSP*

Under the original SSP scheme the employer was able to recoup 100 per cent of the SSP paid out to employees. Indeed, under the Social Security Act 1985, the principle of reimbursement was extended to allow the employer to reclaim a further amount in respect of the secondary Class 1 National Insurance contributions he was liable to pay on SSP payments.

From 6 April 1991, the Statutory Sick Pay Act 1991 provided that an employer could only recoup 80 per cent of the amount of SSP which he paid out and removed the provision for reclaiming the allowance for secondary National Insurance contributions.

The Statutory Sick Pay Act 1994 removes the general right for employers to reclaim any SSP paid to employees after April 1995.

(b) *'Small employer's' relief (SER)*

SER was introduced by the Statutory Sick Pay Act 1991, to allow small employers to reclaim at least part of the amount they expended on SSP. The original scheme is replaced by a scheme made under the 1994 Act together with the Statutory Sick Pay Percentage Threshold Order 1995 (SI 1995/512), which came into effect in April 1995. The scheme allows employers to recoup SSP payments from the State to the extent that those payments exceed 13 per cent of the employer's NI contributions for the month in question. The level of 13 per cent was set to equate to the cost of the original SER.

98 Sunday Trading Act 1994

The provisions of Schedule 4 of this Act, which provide for the protection of shop workers in relation to Sunday work, have been repealed and consolidated into the Employment Rights Act 1996.

99 Trade Union Act 1913 (repealed consolidated)

Amended by Industrial Relations Act 1971, Trade Union and Labour Relations Act 1974, Employment Protection Act 1975, Employment Protection (Consolidation) Act 1978, Trade Union Act 1984 and Employment Act 1988 and 1990.

Its remaining provisions were consolidated into TULRA.

100   Trade Union Act 1984 (repealed consolidated)

Amends Employment Act 1980, Trade Union Act 1913, Trade Union and Labour Relations Act 1974. Amended by Employment Acts 1988 and 1990.

Its remaining provisions were consolidated into TULRA.

101   Trade Union (Amalgamations) Act 1964

Deals with the machinery under which trade unions can amalgamate and/or transfer their engagements.

This is repealed/consolidated into TULRA.

102   Trade Union and Labour Relations (Consolidation) Act 1992 (TULRA)

Consolidates the law relating to trade unions from the following statutes: Conspiracy and Protection of Property Act 1875, Trade Union Act 1913, Industrial Courts Act 1919, Trade Union (Amalgamations, etc.) Act 1964, Industrial Relations Act 1971, Trade Union and Labour Relations Act 1974, Trade Union and Labour Relations (Amendment) Act 1976, Employment Protection Act 1975, Employment Protection (Consolidation) Act 1978, Interpretation Act 1978, Reserve Forces Act 1980, Employment Acts 1980–1990, Trade Union Act 1984, Companies Consolidation (Consequential Provisions) Act 1985, Public Order Act 1986.

Amended by TURERA, Collective Redundancies and Transfer of Undertakings (Protection of Employment) (Amendment) Regulations SI 1995/2587 and Employment Rights Act 1996.

102.1   Meaning of 'trade union', list of unions and certification of independence

Originally ss 2, 8 and 30 Trade Union and Labour Relations Act 1974 and s 8 Employment Protection Act 1975.

(a) *Definition of 'trade union'*
   A union is defined as:
   (i)   an organisation consisting of workers of one or more types whose main purposes include the regulation of relations between workers of that type and employers or employers' associations; or
   (ii) an organisation whose members are trade unions (such as the TUC).

(b) *List of trade unions*
   (i)   The Certification Officer keeps a list of trade unions. Organisations wishing to be registered as trade unions can apply to the Certification Officer. They must provide him with
   ● a copy of the rules of the organisation
   ● a list of its officers
   ● the address of its head or main office
   ● the name by which it is, or is to be, known, and
   ● the prescribed fee.

(ii)   If the Certification Officer is satisfied that the organisation is a trade union, that they have fulfilled the above requirements and are not using a name which belongs to, or which has been used by, another registered trade union, then he must enter them onto the list of trade unions.

(iii) The Certification Officer also has certain powers to strike unions off the list he holds.

(c) *Independent trade unions*

(i)   The majority of employment law rights conferred on trade unions have been restricted to those unions which are independent. A trade union is defined as independent if
- it is not under the domination or control of one or more employers or employers' associations, and
- it is not liable to interference by any employer/s or employers' associations (from the provision of financial or material support or other means tending towards such control).

(ii)   A trade union which is on the list of trade unions can apply to the Certification Officer for a certificate of independence.

(iii) The Certification Officer can withdraw a union's certificate of independence if he is of the opinion that the union is no longer independent. If he does this, however, the union can appeal against his decision.

102.2 Status and property of trade unions

(a) *Status of trade unions*

Although trade unions are not corporate bodies they have power to make contracts and to sue and to be sued in their own right. Their objects which might otherwise be considered to be void as being in restraint of trade (since, for example, their objects might include preventing people from working) are specifically declared by statute not to offend against the general common law principles outlawing agreements which are in restraint of trade.

(b) *Property of trade unions*

(i)   The property of trade unions must be vested in trustees. The trustees can be personally liable, and can be sued by individual members of the union, if they misuse union property.

(ii)   It is unlawful for a trade union to use any of its property to pay for any penalty imposed on a union member by a court. If a union does make any such payment then it is under an obligation to recoup it and an individual member is entitled to force the union to pursue recoupment.

(iii) Death benefits
- Unions may pay sums of up to £5,000 on the death of a member.
- Members can nominate their beneficiaries under these provisions.

(c) *Liability in tort*

The liability of unions in tort is dealt with under industrial action (*see below*).

102.3   Trade union administration

(a) *Register of members*

Unions are required to keep an up-to-date register of their members, including their home or work addresses. Where the names on the register are required to be given to an outsider, such as a scrutineer in relation to elections for certain union offices, the union is required to impose a duty of confidentiality on that person as regards the information on the register. This requirement was brought in by TURERA.

(b) *Duty to supply rules*

Unions are required to supply any person with a copy of its rules either free of charge or on payment of a reasonable fee.

(c) *Accounting records*

   (i)   Unions are required to prepare accounts and to keep them available for inspection for six years. Union members can inspect any such accounts, with their accountants if desired, for the time for which they have been members of the union.

   (ii) Unions are required to appoint auditors and to send annual returns to the Certification Officer. At the same time as sending an annual return to the Certification Officer unions are required to send an annual statement to members – broadly similar to a company's annual return. This, latter, amendment was introduced by TURERA.

102.4   Elections for trade union officers

(a) *Who must be elected*

The president, general secretary and members of the executive of a union must be re-elected every five years. This does not apply to long-serving members of the executive who are within five years of retirement and who would otherwise be allowed by the union rules to stay on until retirement without being re-elected.

(b) *The election process*

   (i)   No union member may be unreasonably excluded from standing for election.

   (ii) Each candidate is allowed to prepare an election address in his own words. The candidates' election addresses must be distributed by the union.

   (iii) The union must appoint an independent scrutineer to oversee the election.

   (iv) Generally, each union member must be given the same right to vote, but the union is entitled to exclude certain categories, such as those who are unemployed or in arrears with their subscriptions, or to limit the vote to certain classes of member within the union (eg to those within a particular geographical location or to members of a particular trade).

   (v)   Each eligible member has a right to vote in a secret postal ballot. The votes must be counted by an independent person (this is a TURERA amendment) and there must be a scrutineer's report produced saying that the scrutineer is satisfied with the way in which the election has been conducted. The results of the election cannot be published until the scrutineer's report has OK'd the election. The union must send a copy or inform all members of the terms of the scrutineer's report within three months of receiving it. By amendments added by TURERA the scrutineer is also required to examine the union's register of members and to satisfy himself that it is accurate and up to date.

102.5   Use of funds for political objectives

(a) *Political fund resolution*

A union's funds cannot be used for political purposes, as defined by the Act, unless:

(i)   The union has adopted a political resolution. Such a resolution must be approved by a majority of those voting in a ballot and the political resolution must be re-balloted every 10 years.

(ii)   The union must make payments for political objectives out of a separate fund from which members can be exempted from contributing.

(iii) The union's rules regarding the use of funds for political purposes must be approved by the Certification Officer.

(b) *Members' contributions to political funds*

(i)   When a union adopts a political resolution it must tell its members of that fact. It must also tell them that they are entitled to be exempted from contributing to the political fund. They must be told that they can obtain an exemption notice, exempting them from political fund contributions from the union's Head Office or from the Certification Officer. Section 84 sets out a statutory form of exemption notice which can be used by members not wishing to contribute to the political fund.

(ii)   If an employee, who has union subscriptions deducted from his pay under the check-off system, is exempt from making political fund contributions and notifies his employer of this in writing then:

● the employer must not deduct political fund contributions from that employee's pay; and

● the employer must not refuse to make deductions under the check-off system in respect of the employee while he continues to make check-off deductions for other employees (unless his refusal has nothing to do with the fact that the employee is exempt from making political fund contributions).

(iii) Where the employer either:

● makes deductions despite the employee being exempt from contributing to the political fund; or

● refuses to continue to make deductions of the employee's union sub-

scriptions after being notified that the employee is exempt from contributing to the union's political fund

the employee can apply to the county court (sheriff's court in Scotland)
which can make a declaration if it finds for the employee.

(iv) If the employee's complaint is that the employer has made unlawful
deductions from his pay – by making deductions in respect of the political fund contribution when the employee was exempt – the time for bringing a claim under the s 23 ERA (claim for unlawful deductions from
wages) runs from the date of the declaration by the court of the employee's right not to have had that amount deducted.

102.6 Funding and use of employer's premises for ballots

TULRA originally provided that public funding would be available for certain trade
union ballots, including those for elections of the executive committee, political fund
ballots and industrial action ballots. These provisions were repealed by TURERA with
effect from 1 April 1996. The provisions allowing for the unions to use the employer's
premises to hold such ballots where the employer recognised the union and had
more than 20 employees was also repealed by TURERA with effect from 1 April 1996.
To a large extent using the employer's premises would be of no assistance now since
most types of ballot now require a postal rather than a workplace ballot.

102.7 Employers' Associations

The Act defines Employers' Associations, provides for the Certification Officer to
keep a list of them, deals with the status and property of Employers' Associations
and their administration, ability to apply funds for political objectives and for amalgamations and similar matters.

102.8 Rights of trade union members against the union

(a) *Rights on unballoted union action*

TULRA allows a trade union member to bring an action against the union
where the union has authorised or endorsed any industrial action which has
not been approved by a secret ballot. A member can only bring an action if
members of the union (including the complainant himself), have been or are
likely to be induced to take part in, or to continue, the 'unapproved' industrial
action.

This provision gives individual union members the right to complain that the
trade union has failed to hold a proper ballot or to obtain a vote in favour of the
industrial action as a result of that ballot (*see 'Industrial action' below*).
Originally only employers were in a position to complain about a union's failure to obtain the sanction of a ballot before taking industrial action. This extension, to allow individual trade union members to complain of unballoted
strike action, was originally brought into effect by the Employment Act 1988.

(b) *Access to the courts for members*

Where a trade union member has applied for any matter to be determined in accordance with the trade union's rules and that matter has not been dealt with within six months, then, regardless of anything in the union rules, the member can take his grievance to court. There are provisions which allow this six-month period to be extended where the reason for the union failing to deal with the issue was the member's own fault.

If the individual's application to the union to deal with any matter is invalid then the union must inform him, within 28 days of the application, of the ways in which the application is invalid. If the union fails to do this then the member is entitled to treat his application as validly made.

(c) *Right not to be unjustifiably disciplined*

A trade union member/former member is given the right not to be unjustifiably disciplined by the union. It is unjustifiable for a union to discipline someone because he is or is believed to be guilty of any of the following:

(i)   not supporting, or indicating opposition to, or lack of support for, a strike or other industrial action

(ii)   not breaching an agreement between himself and his employer to support a strike or other industrial action (NB The wording of this makes it clear that this is not limited to *employees* who are trade union members.)

(iii) asserting, or vindicating someone else's assertion, that the union or any official or representative of the union or a trustee of any union property has or proposes to contravene any agreement, union rule or rule of law, or consulting the Trade Union Commissioner or the Certification Officer in respect of any such matter – unless the member is acting in bad faith in making or vindicating an assertion which he believes to be false

(iv)   encouraging or helping someone else not to breach their agreement with *their* employer

(v)   failing to agree, or withdrawing agreement, to deductions being made from his wages in respect of union dues

(vi)   resigning or proposing to resign from a union, becoming or proposing to become a member of another union or refusing to become a member of another union

(vii) working with, or proposing to work with, non-union members

(viii) working for, or proposing to work for, an employer who employs or who has employed non-union members, whether of the particular union or of another union, or

(ix)   requiring the union to do anything which the union is required by TULRA to do if asked by a member.

Unjustifiable discipline in this context includes:

   • expulsion, from the union or from a branch of it

Items (v) to (ix) above were added by TURERA.

- a fine of any sort
- withdrawal of any of the services or benefits of membership
- any other detriment.

Complaints under these provisions must be presented to an industrial tribunal within three months of the decision which gave rise to the complaint.

If the tribunal finds the complaint well founded it will make a declaration to that effect. The applicant can then apply to the tribunal if the union's decision has been withdrawn and it has done all it can to ensure a reversal of the effects of that decision or to Employment Appeal Tribunal (EAT) if those steps have not been taken.

Any such application cannot be made earlier than four weeks after the tribunal's declaration. In these, later, proceedings the tribunal or EAT can:

- order repayment of any sums the member has paid out under the union's decision; and
- award such compensation as it considers 'just and equitable in all the circumstances of the case', subject to the total not exceeding the maximum basic award plus the maximum compensatory award which could be obtained in an unfair dismissal case. If the application is brought to the EAT then the *minimum* award is the same as the 'special' basic award which is awarded where an employee has been dismissed for an inadmissible reason (*see Employment Rights Act 1996 – unfair dismissal remedies*).

(d) *Right to terminate union membership*

Every union member has the right to terminate his union membership on giving reasonable notice and complying with any reasonable conditions.

(e) *Right not to be excluded or expelled from union*

The Employment Act 1980 provided a right for employees who were in 'closed shop' employment not to be unreasonably expelled or excluded from the trade unions who were party to the closed shop agreement. (A 'closed shop' meant that only members of the appropriate unions could be employed in that employment.) TURERA has extended this protection, in modified form, to protect all trade union members and would-be trade union members from being excluded from or expelled by a trade union other than on certain specific grounds.

(i) *The right*

The grounds on which a person *can* be excluded or expelled from a trade union are:

- if the person no longer meets an 'enforceable membership requirement'. An 'enforceable membership requirement' is one which restricts membership by reference purely to:
  - employment in a specified trade, industry or profession
  - occupational description (including grade, level or category of appointment); or

- possession of specific trade, industrial or professional qualifications or work experience
- if the person is not within the geographical area in which the union operates
- where the union operates within a single company or within a group of associated companies, if the person ceases to be employed by the company/group
- where the exclusion or expulsion is solely because of the individual's conduct. But there are certain types of conduct which it is not permissible to expel or exclude an individual for. These are:
  - the individual being or ceasing to be
    - a member of another trade union
    - employed by a particular employer or at a particular place, or
    - a member of a political party, or
  - conduct in relation to any trade union for which, under the Act (*see (c) above*), an individual may not be disciplined by a trade union.

(ii) Remedies
- A complaint made be made to a tribunal within six months of the date of expulsion or exclusion from the union or, if that is not reasonably practicable, within such further time as is reasonably practicable.
- Where the tribunal finds the claim to be substantiated it must make a declaration to that effect.
- Compensation
  - If the employee is admitted/re-admitted by the union, then the compensation claim is heard by an industrial tribunal otherwise the claim is dealt with by the EAT.
  - The claim, in either case, must be made within four weeks of the tribunal's declaration.
  - The amount of compensation awarded is such as is considered just and equitable and a reduction can be made for any contributory conduct on the part of the applicant.
  - The maximum award which can be made is:
    - 30 weeks' pay (subject to the statutory upper limit for a 'week's pay'); plus
    - the maximum compensatory award for unfair dismissal.
    - Where the EAT makes the award the minimum award is £5,000 (and this appears, from the wording of the section, to be after any reduction for contributory fault has been taken into account).

(f) *Commissioner for the Rights of Trade Union Members*
Assistance can be sought by individual union members from the Commissioner for the Rights of Trade Union Members to enforce many of the members' rights under the Act. In considering whether or not to provide assistance or how much assistance to provide in any particular case the things

which the Commissioner for the Rights of Trade Union Members can take into account include:

(i)   whether the case raises any question of principle

(ii) whether the case is too complex reasonably to expect the applicant to deal with it unaided, and

(iii) whether the Commissioner considers the case to involve a matter of substantial public interest.

102.9 Rights of trade union members in relation to employment

(a) *Right to require employer to stop deductions of union subscriptions*

This more extensive right was substituted by TURERA. The original requirement was that if an employee informed his employer that he had left the union with effect from a particular date then the employer must stop checking off union dues from that date or as soon thereafter as is reasonably practicable.

(i)   The new right requires an employer:

- not to make any union subscription deduction which is not authorised; and

- to ensure that any subscription deduction which is made is not more than the authorised amount.

(ii) To be authorised, permission to make the subscription deduction must be

- authorised in a written document which is:

  - signed and dated by the worker

  - no more than three years old at the date when the deduction is made.

- Where the authorisation has been withdrawn then no deductions may be made after the withdrawal has been received by the employer (subject to there being enough time after the date of the withdrawal for it to be reasonably practicable to stop the deductions being made from the payment in question).

(iii) The amount which an employer is authorised to deduct is the amount covered by the subscription deduction arrangement. Where there is any increase in subscription then the employer is required to give at least a month's notice before subscriptions can be deducted at a new higher rate.

The 'notice' given to union members for these purposes must tell them:

- of the new subscription level; and

- of the fact that they can withdraw their authorisation to having union subscriptions deducted at any time.

(iv) An employee can complain to an industrial tribunal that an employer has made unauthorised or excessive deductions within three months of the deduction in question or, where that is not reasonably practicable, within such further time as is reasonably practicable.

(v)   (For the right of union members not to have unauthorised Political Fund contributions deducted from their pay and for their right to continue to have the remainder of their union subscriptions deducted by the employer after they have elected not to contribute to the political fund (*see* '*Use of funds for political objectives*' *above, section 102.5*).

(b) *Discriminatory recruitment on 'trade union grounds'*

   (i)   Refusing employment

- The Act provides that it is unlawful for a person to be refused employment on 'trade union grounds'. This makes it unlawful for an employer to refuse to employ a person because either:
  - he is or is not a member of a trade union
  - he is unwilling to accept a requirement to remain, or to become, or to cease to be, a union member
  - or he refuses to have money deducted from his pay as an alternative to being a union member, etc.
- Where there is an arrangement whereby employment is only offered to people put forward by a trade union, then an applicant who applies for and is refused employment because of this practice is deemed to have been refused employment on trade union grounds.
- The Act contains an extended definition of 'refusing employment' which includes:
  - failing to entertain the applicant's application or enquiry, or causing him to withdraw it
  - refusing to offer the applicant employment
  - offering the job on terms which no one who wanted to fill the post would offer
  - offering it on condition that the employee must meet the 'trade union' requirement (eg by joining or leaving the union); or
  - offering the job and then withdrawing that offer.

   (ii) Discriminatory advertising

Where an advertisement is published which indicates, or which might reasonably be understood as indicating, that the employer will require the successful applicant to be or to become a trade union member or to cease to be one, then an employee who applies for and is refused employment is *conclusively* presumed to have been refused employment on trade union grounds if:

- he either does not meet that requirement; or
- he is unwilling to accept that requirement.

This is particularly stringent since it imposes strict liability on an employer in such cases.

  (iii) Discrimination by an employment agency

There are provisions equivalent to items (i) and (ii) above relating to employment agencies. These make it unlawful for an employment agency either to refuse to offer its services on trade union grounds, or to publish a discriminatory advertisement.

For these purposes a trade union is not to be considered as an employment agency in relation to services provided for its members.

(iv)   Union membership requirements in contracts for supply of goods or services

- Any term or condition in a contract for the supply of goods or services which requires the work to be carried out by union members is declared void. Similarly, any term which requires an employer to recognise, consult with or negotiate with a trade union is also void.
- It is unlawful to refuse to deal with any supplier of goods or services on grounds relating to the trade union status of any of that supplier's employees. It is also unlawful to refuse to deal with a supplier on the grounds that they recognise, consult or negotiate with a trade union (or because they do not do so).

(v)   Remedy

- *Time limit*

A complaint may be made to an industrial tribunal within three months of the discrimination in question. The type of case where problems can immediately be envisaged, in terms of trying to determine when the discrimination actually occurred, is where an employer has simply omitted to offer employment. In such a case the Act provides that time for application is to run from 'the end of the period within which it was reasonable to expect the employer to act'. This may lead to some interesting case law.

- *Remedies*

The industrial tribunal can order the employer to pay compensation which is to be assessed in the same way as compensation for breach of statutory duty (and which can include compensation for injury to feelings). The maximum amount of compensation which can be awarded is the same as the maximum unfair dismissal compensatory award (£11,300).

In addition to a monetary award the tribunal can recommend that the respondent takes specific action to obviate or reduce the adverse effect on the applicant of the conduct complained of. If the respondent fails to take the recommended action the tribunal can award compensation or greater compensation to reflect that failure. The total award, however, is still subject to the overall maximum of £11,300.

- *Joinder of third parties*

Where the employer's conduct was to any extent caused by a third party exercising pressure by threatening to call a strike or to take other industrial action, that third party (which will usually be a trade union) can be joined to the proceedings. In such cases the tribunal can make a compensatory award against either or both parties and in such proportions as it sees fit. Where the case could be brought against an employer or an employment agency and the union member takes action against only one then the other can be joined at the instance of either party and any compensation can again be awarded against either or both in such proportions as the tribunal considers just in the circumstances.

(c) *Action short of dismissal*
  (i) The prohibition
       An employer is not allowed to take action short of dismissal against an employee:
       - to prevent or deter him from or to penalise him for:
         - being a member of; or
         - taking part, at an appropriate time, in the activities of an independent trade union. (An 'appropriate time' for taking part in trade union activities for these purposes is outside working hours or during working hours at times when by agreement or arrangement with the employer it is permissible to take part in union activities.)
       - to compel him to be a member of a trade union
       - to enforce a requirement to pay an amount in lieu of union dues for non-union members.
  (ii) Exclusion for personal contracts
       Where an employee is offered an inducement to enter into a personal contract (ie to enter into a separately negotiated agreement with his employer rather than accepting the terms which have been collectively agreed with the union) then this is expressly declared by statute not to be action short of dismissal against a person who does not accept this inducement (unless no employer could reasonably use the inducement in question to try to change his contractual relationship with his employees – for example, offering to pay non-union members double what was negotiated with the union under the collective agreement). This amendment was brought in by TURERA although the cases which it was introduced to overrule have since been overruled by the House of Lords on appeal.
  (iii) The remedy
       An employee can bring a claim at any time within three months of the action in question (with a provision to extend this time limit if it cannot reasonably be met). Where there is a series of actions giving rise to the complaint then it is the last that the three-month time limit runs from.
       No account is to be taken of any pressure placed on the employer to take the action complained of. Any third party can be joined to the proceedings and the tribunal can make an award against the third party to the extent that is just and equitable.
(d) *Dismissal for trade union reasons*
  (i) The prohibition
       The dismissal or selection for redundancy of an employee on grounds of trade union membership or taking part in trade union activities is to be regarded as unfair. Such dismissals are considered to be for an inadmissible reason. Inadmissible reasons for dismissal are:
       - because the employee was or proposed to become a member of an independent trade union

- because the employee had or proposed to take part in the activities of an independent trade union at an appropriate time. (An 'appropriate time' for taking part in trade union activities for these purposes is outside working hours or during working hours at times when by agreement or arrangement with the employer it is permissible to take part in union activities); or
- because he was not a member of a union or of a particular trade union
- because he refused to agree to allow his employer to deduct an amount in lieu of union dues from his pay.

(ii)   Remedies

The remedies in a case of unfair dismissal or unfair selection for redundancy on grounds of trade union membership or activities are the same as those for 'special cases' of unfair dismissal under ERA. There is also a facility to join third parties to proceedings and a provision for interim relief to be provided to allow for the contract of employment to be continued pending the outcome of the tribunal case (*see also ERA: 'Protection for health and safety representatives, trustees of pension schemes and employee representatives' above, section 36.6, where these remedies are dealt with in more detail*).

(e) *Time off for trade union duties*

(i)   The right

- An employee who is an official of a recognised independent trade union is entitled not to be unreasonably refused paid time off during working hours for:
  - negotiations with the employer about:
    - things falling within the statutory definition of collective bargaining (*see 'Industrial relations, collective bargaining' below*)
    - in respect of the which the union is recognised by the employer
  - the performance of functions which the employer has agreed may be performed by the union related to
    - things falling within the statutory definition of collective bargaining (*see 'Industrial relations, collective bargaining' below*)
    - in respect of the which the union is recognised by the employer
  - training to enable the official to carry out the above duties provided that the training is approved by the TUC or by the independent trade union of which he is an official.
- The amount of time off which is to be permitted and the reasons for it are subject to what is reasonable and to the terms of an ACAS Code of Practice.

(ii)   Remedy

A trade union official who is unreasonably refused paid time off or who is not paid for it can complain to an industrial tribunal within three months of the incident or within such further time as is reasonably practicable if it is not reasonably practicable to meet the three-month time limit. Where the tribunal finds that the official has not been paid where he should have been it must award payment for time off which should have been given; it may also award compensation for the failure to give time off.

(f) *Time off for trade union activities*
   (i) The right
      • An employee who is a member of a recognised independent trade union is entitled to reasonable time off during working hours to take part in:
         • any activities of the union; and
         • any activities of the union in relation to which he is an official or representative of the union.
      • The amount of time off which is to be permitted and the reasons for it are subject to what is reasonable and to the terms of an ACAS Code of Practice.
   (ii) Remedy
      A trade union member who is unreasonably refused time off for trade union activities can complain to an industrial tribunal within three months of the incident or within such further time as is reasonably practicable if it is not reasonably practicable to meet the three-month time limit. On an application the tribunal may make an award of compensation for time off which should have been given.

102.10   Procedure for handling redundancies

Until 1995 the right to have representatives consulted in relation to redundancies would have been seen as a right accorded to trade union members. TURERA and the Collective Redundancies and Transfer of Undertakings (Protection of Employment) (Amendment) Regulations 1995 SI 1995/2587, which were brought in to give effect to requirements under Council Directive 92/56/EEC and to deal with the shortfall in the way in which the UK had dealt with its original obligations in respect of collective redundancies under Council Directive 75/129/EEC (the Collective Redundancies Directives), have had the effect of extending these provisions both in relation to when and how consultation must occur and in terms of requiring consultation where unions are not recognised.

(a) *Extended meaning of redundancy for consultation purposes and presumption of redundancy*
   For purposes of the consultation requirements, 'dismissal for redundancy' is widely defined as meaning dismissal for a reason or reasons not related to the individual concerned. It is presumed that any proposal to dismiss an employee is because of redundancy, in this extended sense, unless the employer shows the dismissal to be for some other reason.

(b) *Consultation*
  (i)   Circumstances in which required and timing
    • Where an employer is proposing to dismiss 20 or more employees at one establishment within a period of 90 days or less then he must consult with the appropriate representative of those employees at least 30 days before the first dismissal takes effect.
    • Where the employer is proposing to dismiss more than 100 employees at one establishment within a period of 90 days then he must start consultations at least 90 days before the first dismissal takes effect.
    • In considering the numbers of employees being dismissed, no account is to be taken of employees in respect of whom consultation has already begun.
    • These provisions do not apply to those who are employed
      • under a contract for a fixed term of three months or less, or
      • under a contract to perform a specific task which is not expected to last for more than three months
    provided that the employee/s in question have not been continuously employed for more than three months.
    • Where there are special circumstances which make it not reasonably practicable for the employer to start consultations with employee representatives on time then he must do what he can towards meeting these requirements. (It is no excuse if the employer's decision to make redundancies has been taken by someone who controls the employer (such as a holding company) and that person has not given the employer information which he needs to start consultations.)
  (ii) Employee representatives
    • Where there is a recognised independent trade union then the employer can chose to consult either representatives of that independent trade union or employee representatives. If no independent union is recognised then the employer must consult employee representatives.
    • The employer may consult employee representatives either
      • who have been elected by employees specifically to be consulted with their employer about proposed redundancy dismissals; or
      • who were elected by employees for other purposes and who are considered appropriate (having regard to the purposes for which they were elected) for the employer to consult about proposed dismissals.
    They must also be employed by the employer at the time when they were elected.
    • If
      • the employer invites any of the employees who may be dismissed in a redundancy exercise to elect employee representatives; and
      • that invitation is made long enough before the time when consultation needs to begin to allow for employee representatives to be elected by the beginning of the obligatory consultation period

then the employer is deemed to have complied with his statutory consultation obligations if he fulfils those obligations as soon as is reasonably practicable after the representatives are elected.
- An employer must allow employee representatives:
  - access to the employees whom it is proposed to make redundant; and
  - accommodation and such other facilities as may be appropriate.
(iii) Starting consultation
- To begin consultation, the employer must disclose the following matters in writing to the appropriate representatives:
  - the reasons for his proposals
  - the numbers and descriptions of employees whom it is proposed to dismiss as redundant
  - the total number of employees of any such description employed by the employer at the establishment in question
  - the proposed method of selecting the employees who may be dismissed
  - the proposed method of carrying out the dismissals, with due regard to any agreed procedure, including the period over which the dismissals are to take effect; and
  - the proposed method of calculating the amount of any redundancy payments in excess of the statutory which are to be made to those who are made redundant.
- The above information must be given to appropriate representatives by being given or sent to them by post.
- The employer must also provide employee representatives with a copy of any notice which the employer is required to give to the Secretary of State regarding the redundancies *(see (d) below)*.
- Where there are special circumstances which make it not reasonably practicable for the employer to give the employee representatives this information or to give it to them on time then he must do what he can towards meeting these requirements. It is no excuse if the employer's decision to make redundancies has been taken by someone who controls the employer (such as a holding company) and that person has not given the employer any of the information he needs for these purposes.
(iv) What consultation involves
- Consultation must be undertaken by the employer with a view to reaching agreement with the appropriate representatives on matters including ways of:
  - avoiding the dismissals
  - reducing the numbers of employees to be dismissed, and
  - mitigating the consequences of the dismissals

- Where there are special circumstances which make it not reasonably practicable to fulfil these requirements then the employer must do what he can towards meeting them. (It is no excuse if the employer's decision to make redundancies has been taken by someone who controls the employer (such as a holding company) and that person has failed to provide the employer with any information he may require.)

(c) *Protective award*

   (i)   Protective award

- A protective award is made in respect of:
  - employees who have been dismissed, or whom it is proposed to dismiss, as redundant; and
  - in respect of whom the consultation requirements have not been fully complied with.

  The order requires the employer to pay the employees their remuneration during the protected period. (Employees who are employed during the protective period are only entitled to remuneration if they are entitled to it under their contracts or if they are entitled to it as payment for their statutory notice period under the ERA.)
- The protected period begins with the earlier of:
  - the date on which the first of the dismissals takes effect; or
  - the date of the award.
- The protected period continues for such time as the tribunal considers just and equitable having regard to the seriousness of the employer's default but can be no longer than
  - 90 days where it was proposed to dismiss more than 100 employees at one establishment as redundant within 90 days; or
  - 30 days where it was proposed to dismiss between 20 and 100 employees at one establishment as redundant within 90 days.
- Where an employee is entitled to be paid under a protective award and the employer fails to pay then the employee can bring a claim to an industrial tribunal within three months of that failure, or such longer time as is reasonably practicable, where it is not reasonably practicable to meet the three-month limit.

   (ii)   Who may claim a protective award and when

- The appropriate claimant where an employer has not fulfilled the consultation requirements depends on the employer's particular failure. Where an employer has failed
  - to fulfil any requirement relating to an employee representative, the employee representative
  - to fulfil any requirement relating to a trade union representative, the trade union
  - in any other case an employee who has been or may be dismissed as redundant.
- A claim must be brought either:

- before the last dismissal to which the claim relates; or
- within three months of the last dismissal (or if that is not reasonably practicable within such further period as is reasonably practicable).
- If the tribunal finds the claim to be founded then it must make a declaration to that effect. It may also make a protective award.

(iii) Termination of employment during protected period

- If the employee is fairly dismissed (other than for redundancy) or unreasonably terminates his employment during the protective period then his right to be paid under the protective award ceases when his employment ends.
- Where an employee is offered suitable alternative employment whilst still employed he will lose his right to be paid under the protective award if he unreasonably refuses the offer. His entitlement to be paid under the protective award will cease from the time when the alternative employment would have started and he is, instead, dismissed or leaves.
- An employee who takes alternative employment on a trial basis and unreasonably terminates his employment during the trial period will lose his right to be paid under the protective award from the time when his employment ends.

(d) *Notifying Secretary of State of redundancies*

- Where the employer is proposing to dismiss more than 100 employees at one establishment within a period of 90 days then he must notify the Secretary of State of his proposals at least 90 days before the first dismissal takes effect.
- Where an employer is proposing to dismiss between 20 and 100 employees at one establishment within a period of 90 days then he must notify the Secretary of State of his proposals at least 30 days before the first dismissal takes effect.
- In considering the numbers of employees being dismissed, no account is taken of employees in respect of whom a notice has already been given to the Secretary of State.
- A notice under this requirement must be in a form specified by the Secretary of State and after receiving it the Secretary of State can ask for such further information as he may require.
- Where there are special circumstances which make it not reasonably practicable for the employer to notify the Secretary of State on time then he must do what he can towards meetings these requirements. (It is no excuse if the employer's decision to make redundancies has been taken by someone who controls the employer (such as a holding company) and that person has not given the employer information which he needs to notify the Secretary of State.)
- It is an offence to fail to notify the Secretary of State, or to fail to notify him on time. The company and any manager, officer or secretary responsible can be convicted of the failure.

(e) *Collective agreements*
- Where there is a collective agreement in force which establishes
  - agreements for providing alternative employment for employees if they are dismissed as redundant; or
  - arrangements for handling the dismissal of employees as redundant
- if the terms of the agreement are at least as beneficial to employees as the statutory consultation provisions then the parties can apply to the Secretary of State to be exempted from the statutory consultation requirements.

102.11   Collective bargaining

(a) *Collective agreements*
    (i)   Definitions
- A 'Collective agreement' is an agreement about any matter which can be the subject of collective bargaining (*see below*). To be a collective agreement the agreement must be reached between trades union/s and employer/s or employers' associations.
- 'Collective bargaining' means negotiations relating to or connected with one or more of the following:
  - terms and conditions of employment
  - physical conditions in which any workers are required to work
  - engagement/non-engagement, termination or suspension
    - of employment; or
    - of the duties of employment
    of one or more workers
  - allocation of work or the duties of employment between workers or groups of workers
  - matters of discipline
  - a worker's membership or non-membership of a trade union
  - facilities for officials of trade unions
  - machinery for negotiation or consultation
  - other procedures, relating to any of the above matters, including recognition by an employer of the right of a trade union to represent workers in such negotiations or consultation or in the carrying out of such procedures.
- 'Recognition' means recognition to any extent for collective bargaining purposes.
- 'Trade dispute' has two separate meanings – one for purposes of collective bargaining and the duties of ACAS which is considerably wider than the second which is used for purposes of deciding whether or not a trade union is immune from action in tort in respect of industrial action taken by its members. Both of these definitions are dealt with below, the first under 'Arbitration, mediation and conciliation' and the second under 'Industrial action'.

(ii)   Legal enforceability
   • A collective agreement is conclusively presumed not to be legally bind-
     ing unless:
       • it contains a provision, however expressed, saying that the parties
         intend it to be legally enforceable; and
       • it is in writing.
   • A term in a collective agreement which prohibits or restricts the right
     of workers to take strike or other industrial action cannot form part of
     the worker's contract of employment unless the following conditions
     are met.
       • The collective agreement must
         – be in writing
         – expressly say that those terms can be incorporated into the
           worker's contract
         – be reasonably accessible at the worker's place of work for him to
           consult during working hours; and
         – be one where each trade union which is a party to the agreement
           is an independent trade union; and
         the worker's contract must expressly or impliedly incorporate those
         terms of the collective agreement.
       • Where the above criteria are met then the 'no strike' provisions take
         effect notwithstanding:
         – the general proposition that collective agreements are unenforce-
           able; and
         – despite any provision to the contrary in any agreement (including
           a collective agreement or a contract with any worker).
   • NB: even if a 'no-strike' agreement is enforceable, an employee still
     cannot be forced by a court either to work or to attend at any place to
     do any work. The employer's only remedy against the employee will be
     in damages or to dismiss the employee.
(b) *Disclosure of information for collective bargaining*
   (i)   General requirement
       • An employer who recognises an independent trade union must dis-
         close information to that union's representatives, if they ask for it. The
         trade union representatives can request information for purposes of
         collective bargaining about matters for which the union is recognised
         by the employer. Subject to this, the types of information which may be
         requested are:
           • information without which the trade union representatives would be
             materially hampered in their collective bargaining with the em-
             ployer, and
           • those which it would be good industrial relations practice for the em-
             ployer to disclose to them for collective bargaining purposes.
       • When considering what it is 'good industrial relations practice to dis-

close' the provisions of the ACAS Code of Practice on Disclosure of Information must be taken into account, but not to the exclusion of any other evidence of what good practice is.

- The employer can ask for the union's request for disclosure to be in writing, or to be confirmed in writing and the union can ask for the information to be in writing, or to be confirmed in writing.

(ii) Limitations on duty of disclosure

- An employer is not required to disclose information for collective bargaining purposes:
  - where disclosure would be against the interests of national security
  - which he could not disclose without contravening a statutory prohibition
  - which has been communicated to him in confidence, or obtained as a result of a confidence being entrusted to him by another person
  - which relates specifically to an individual (unless that individual has consented to its being disclosed)
  - where disclosure would cause substantial injury to the employer's undertaking for reasons other than its effect on collective bargaining
  - where the information was obtained by the employer for the purpose of bringing, prosecuting or defending any legal proceedings.

- Nor is an employer required:
  - to produce, make copies, or allow inspection of any document (other than a document prepared for the purpose of conveying or confirming the information)
  - to compile or assemble any information where the cost or work involved in compiling or assembling that information would be out of reasonable proportion to the value of the information in collective bargaining terms.

(iii) Complaints of failure to disclose

- A trade union can complain to the Central Arbitration Committee (CAC) that:
  - an employer has failed to disclose collective bargaining information; or
  - has failed to confirm that information in writing.

- The CAC refers such cases to ACAS for conciliation where possible or, if conciliation is not possible or has failed, the CAC hears the case. Where the CAC determines the case in favour of the union then it must make a declaration and give the employer a date not less than a week later by which the employer must disclose the information or in which to confirm the disclosed information in writing.

- If the employer fails to comply with the CAC's decision the union can put in a further claim and can ask the CAC to make an award modifying the terms and conditions of relevant employees. The CAC can, on hearing the matter, award the terms and conditions claimed or such other terms and conditions as it considers appropriate.

(c) *Codes of practice*
- ACAS can issue Codes of Practice containing practical guidance aimed at improving industrial relations.
- The Secretary of State may issue Codes of Practice containing practical guidance aimed at:
  - improving industrial relations, or
  - promoting good practice in relation to the way in which trade unions conduct ballots and elections.
- Any failure to follow any of these Codes of Practice does not give rise to any liability in itself, but may be taken into account by a tribunal, court or CAC as evidence in any case.

(d) *Arbitration, mediation and conciliation*
  (i) ACAS
  - ACAS's general duty is to promote the improvement of industrial relations, particularly by helping to settle trade disputes. Under an amendment made by TURERA, ACAS can offer advice to workers, employers and trade unions or may publish advice on industrial relations issues. ACAS, under the TURERA amendments, is now also able to charge for its advice.
  - Where there is a trade dispute ACAS can at the request of either party offer conciliation or mediation by an independent third party.
  - Where there is a trade dispute ACAS can at the request of one of the parties and with the consent of all of the parties, refer the matter to arbitration by arbitrators appointed by ACAS or by the CAC. Arbitration should not normally be used unless it is felt that conciliation won't work.
  - ACAS can also involve itself in inquiries into industrial relations generally or in relation to any particular industry where it sees fit to do so.
  (ii) Courts of inquiry
  - Where a trade dispute exists or is anticipated, a Court of Inquiry can be set up by the Secretary of State to look into it.
  (iii) Trade dispute
  - A 'trade dispute' is defined more widely for purposes of the duties of ACAS in relation to trade disputes than it is for the part of the Act which deals with industrial action (*see 102.12(b) below*). For purposes of the duties of ACAS the definition of 'trade dispute'
    - includes a dispute between different sets of workers
    - includes a dispute between workers and any employer
    - includes disputes arising solely outside the UK which have no impact on those taking action in the UK
    - includes disputes involving unions and employers' associations

- but it does not include the mere threat of industrial action which is given in to by the party who or which was threatened.

102.12 Industrial action

(a) *Liability of trade unions in tort*
   (i) General
   - A trade union can only be liable in tort if, the action in question is one which is taken to have been authorised or endorsed by the trade union.
   - An act is taken to have been authorised or endorsed by a trade union if it was done, authorised or endorsed:
     - by a person who is empowered by the union's rules to do, authorise or endorse acts of that kind, or
     - by the principal executive committee, the president or general secretary, or
     - by any other committee of the union, or
     - by any other official of the union who is part of a group whose duties or functions involve organising or co-ordinating industrial action.
   - In relation to the last two groups above, an act is not to be taken as having been authorised or endorsed by virtue of these provisions if it is repudiated by the president, general secretary or executive committee of the union as soon as is reasonably practicable after it comes to the knowledge of any of them.
   (ii) Repudiating an action
   To repudiate an act:
   - written notice must be given to the offending committee or official without delay; and
   - the union must give a written notice to all those who they believe are taking, or might otherwise take, part in industrial action because of the act being repudiated. The notice must contain:
     - the fact of repudiation
     - the date of the repudiation; and
     - the following statement:

       'Your union has repudiated the call (or calls) for industrial action to which this notice relates and will give no support to unofficial industrial action taken in response to it (or them). If you are dismissed while taking unofficial industrial action, you will have no right to complain of unfair dismissal.'

   - Employers of those to whom the above notice is required to be given must also be given written notice of the fact and the date of the repudiation.
   - An act is not, however, to be treated as having been repudiated if, at any time after the purported repudiation the president, general secretary or executive committee do anything inconsistent with that repu-

diation. A person who has a commercial contract (including a contract of employment) which was or which was liable to be interfered with by the repudiated act is given certain rights. Such a person, if he has not already had notice that the act in question has been repudiated can, within three months of the date of the repudiation, ask the union to confirm the repudiation in writing. If the union fails to provide written confirmation of the repudiation 'forthwith', this is to be treated as doing something inconsistent with the repudiation and thus will undermine the effect of the repudiation.

(iii) Limit of trade union liability in tort
- Other than in relation to claims for:
    - personal injury arising out of negligence, nuisance or breach of duty
    - breach of duty in connection with the ownership, occupation, possession, control or use of property; and
    - product liability claims

  the amount of damages awarded against a trade union in any action is limited by the size of the membership of the union.
- The limits are:

Number of members in union	*Maximum damages*
Less than 5,000	£10,000
5,000 – 25,000	£50,000
25,000 – 100,000	£125,000
100,000 or more	£250,000

- Amounts awarded by way of damages cost and expenses against
    - a trade union; or
    - trustees of union property, all the members of a trade union or the officials of a trade union when acting as such

  cannot be recovered from 'protected property'.
- Protected property is:
    - property belonging to the trustees other than in their capacity as such
    - property belonging to any member of the union otherwise than jointly or in common with the other members
    - property belonging to an official of the union who is neither a member nor a trustee
    - property comprised in the union's political fund provided that, at the time of the action complained of, the fund was not allowed to be used for financing strikes or other industrial action
    - property comprised in a separate provident fund including funds to provide benefits:
        - to members during sickness, incapacity from personal injury or accident
        - to members while out of work

- by way of superannuation to aged members
- to members who have lost their tools by fire or theft
- for help with funeral expenses on the death of a member or the wife of a member
- for making provision for the children of a deceased member.

(b) *Action taken in contemplation or furtherance of a trade dispute*

  (i)   Meaning of a trade dispute

  - The definition of a 'trade dispute' for purposes of immunity from liability in tort in relation to industrial action is defined more strictly than it is defined in relation to the duties of ACAS (*see 102.11(d)(i) above*). In relation to industrial action and a union's immunity from action in tort, 'trade dispute' means a dispute between workers and their employer which relates wholly or mainly to one or more of the items which can be the subject of collective bargaining between a union and an employer (*see 'Collective bargaining' – 102.11 (a)(i) above*).
  - A dispute between a Minister of the Crown and any workers is to be treated as a trade dispute if it relates to matters which
    - have been referred for consideration by a joint body on which the Minister is represented, or
    - cannot be settled without him exercising a statutory power.
  - A trade dispute can relate to matters occurring outside the United Kingdom, so long as the people taking action in the United Kingdom are likely to be affected by the outcome of the dispute in respect of one or more of the matters on which a union can collectively bargain with their employer.

  (ii) Protection of action taken in contemplation or furtherance of a trade dispute

  - One of the most important provisions of the Act is that, subject to certain limits, it provides that an act done by a person in contemplation of a trade dispute is not actionable in tort only on the grounds:
    - that it induces another person to break his contract or
    - induces another person to interfere with the performance of a contract; or
    - threatens to do either of the above.
  - This provision is important because it allows for industrial action to be called by a union and taken by employees without exposing them to the possibility of being sued for the torts of: inducement to breach of contract; or interference with the performance of a contract.
  - An *ex parte* injunction/interdict ('ex parte' means that the person against whom the claim is brought is not present or represented at the hearing) must not generally be granted where a person has claimed or is likely to claim that the action which it is sought to restrain is being taken in contemplation or furtherance of a trade dispute. The only exception is where the judge is satisfied that all reasonable steps have

been taken to try to ensure that the defendant has had an opportunity of being heard before the application is decided.
- Where a court is asked to grant an interlocutory injunction in a case where a person claims or is likely to claim that the action was being taken in contemplation or furtherance of a trade dispute, then it must consider the likelihood of that claim succeeding at the full trial before granting an injunction to restrain picketing or inducement to breach or interference with a contract. This does not extend to Scotland.
(iii) Peaceful picketing
  - It is lawful for a person in contemplation or furtherance of a trade dispute to attend:
    - at or near his own place of work
    - where a person works at more than one place or if picketing at his place of work is impracticable, then he can attend at any of his employer's premises from which he works or from which his work is administered
    - if a worker has been dismissed in connection with a trade dispute or if the termination of his employment gave rise to a trade dispute, then he can attend at his former place of work; or
    - if he is a trade union official, at or near the place of work of a member of the union whom
      - he is accompanying; and
      - whom he represents
    - for the purpose of peacefully:
      - obtaining or communicating information, or
      - peacefully persuading any person to work or abstain from working.
  - The ACAS Code of practice on picketing suggests that there should be a maximum of six pickets outside any place of work – although this requirement is advisory only.
  - If picketing goes beyond what is allowed then the immunity from tortious liability is lost and pickets (and if the action is official, the unions) can be sued.
(iv) Actions specifically excluded from protection
  - Action to enforce trade union membership
    - Any action which is taken
      - to enforce a trade union membership requirement for any employees or for people used on contracts; or
      - because an employer has used non-union people
      cannot be protected even if taken in contemplation or furtherance of a trade dispute.
  - Action taken because of dismissal for taking unofficial action
    - An action loses its immunity if it relates, in whole or in part, to people being dismissed for taking unofficial industrial action.
  - Secondary action

- Secondary action occurs where a person
  - induces another to break a contract of employment
  - interferes with the performance of a contract of employment
  - induces another to interfere with its performance
  - threatens that a contract of employment under which he or another is employed will be broken or its performance be interfered with; or
  - threatens that he will induce another to break a contract of employment or to interfere with its performance

  where the employer under the contract of employment is not party to the dispute. Where there are a number of employers in dispute with their workers each dispute between an employer and his workers is treated as a separate dispute.
- Where action is primary action in one dispute (ie where the action is taken by workers against their own employer) then it cannot be outlawed as unlawful secondary action in relation to another dispute.
- Secondary action (other than that which occurs in the course of lawful picketing), is not immune from action in tort.
- Action to impose union recognition
  - Action is not immune from suit in tort if it
    - is taken to make those supplying goods or services use only union labour
    - is taken to try to stop someone obtaining a contract for goods or services because they use or will use non-union labour
    - interferes with the supply or goods or services and is taken by employees not employed by the supplier who believe that the supplier does not or might not recognise a union or consult or negotiate with a union.

(v)   No order to compel work
- It should be noted that even if unlawful action is taken by an employee no order for specific performance or injunction can be made by any court which would compel a person to work or to go anywhere to do work.

(c)   *Ballot requirements before industrial action*

These provisions were extended considerably and amended by TURERA.

(i)   General
- A trade union is not protected against liability for tort in relation to any industrial action unless that action has the support of a ballot *and*
- a trade union is not protected in relation to any particular employer, in respect of industrial action, unless all proper notices and sample voting papers have been given to that employer.
- In the case of a workplace ballot, however, the action will be protected for that workplace if it has the support of a ballot and the proper notices and sample voting papers have been given to that employer which are

valid for employees who work in the place of work in which the ballot is held.
- For an act to have the support of a ballot all the requirements for a valid ballot and proper scrutiny of the ballot must be complied with.

(ii) Scrutiny of the ballot
- A scrutineer must be appointed to oversee an industrial action ballot unless
  - there are 50 or fewer employees who are being balloted; or
  - where there are separate workplace ballots, the average number voting in each workplace ballot is 50 or fewer.
- In all other cases the trade union must:
  - appoint a scrutineer who is competent and of a type or from a list approved by the Secretary of State and who the union has no reason to believe will be biased
  - ensure that the scrutineer carries out his duties in relation to the ballot fully and that he is not subjected to any interference in carrying out those functions from any official, employee or member of the union
  - comply with all reasonable requests made by the scrutineer in carrying out his functions
  - where, within six months of the ballot a person who was entitled to vote in the ballot or an employer of any such person requests a copy of the scrutineer's report the union must provide one as soon as is practicable. (The union can make a reasonable charge for this.)
- The scrutineer's terms of appointment must require him
  - to take such steps as appear to him to be appropriate for the purpose of enabling him to make a scrutineer's report to the union; and
  - to make the report as soon as is reasonably practicable after the date of the ballot and, in any event, within four weeks of the ballot.
- The scrutineer must make a report to the union, following the ballot, which states:
  - that there are no grounds for believing that there has been any breach of statute in relation to the ballot
  - that the arrangements for producing, storing and handling the voting papers used in the ballot, and the arrangements for the counting of the votes, were sufficiently secure to minimise any risk of unfairness or malpractice; and
  - that he has been able to carry out his functions without any interference from the union or any of its members, officials or employees.

  If he is not satisfied as to any of the above, then the report must say what he is dissatisfied with.

(iii) Notice of ballot
- The union must ensure that the employers of those entitled to vote in the ballot receive:
  - not later than the seventh day before a voting paper is sent to anyone entitled to vote in the ballot (ie the 'opening day of the ballot') a notice
    - stating that the union intends to hold the ballot
    - giving the opening day of the ballot, and
    - describing (so the employer can readily identify them) the employees who the union reasonably believes will be entitled to vote in the ballot.
  - not later than the third day before the 'opening day of the ballot' a sample voting paper which must be
    - a sample of the form of voting paper which is to be sent to the employees who are entitled to vote in the ballot, or
    - where different employees are to be given different voting papers, a sample of each.

(iv) Entitlement to vote in ballot
- Entitlement to vote in the ballot must be given to all the union's members who the union believes will be induced to take part or continue to take part in the industrial action in question, and no one else.
- The above requirement is to be taken not to have been satisfied if a person who was a union member at the date of the ballot and who was not given a vote is called upon to take industrial action.
- Where members of a union have different places of work then separate workplace ballots must normally be held to ballot the members of the union working in each separate place of work *but*
  - separate workplace ballots are not used where those who are given the right to vote in the ballot have some factor in common with other union members who are given the right to vote (though the factor they have in common need not be the same factor in each case – so, for example, all the staff employees or blue-collar employees over a number of sites could be balloted together).
    - The factor referred to above must be one which relates to the terms and conditions of those member's employment; or to the occupational description applicable to those members in their employment.
    - The factor must not be one which other employees who are not given a right to vote also have; or which individuals employed by that employer have in common because of their place of work.
- Where a trade union has overseas members then it can decide whether or not to ballot them. Where it does, the scrutiny requirements and many of the other ballot requirements do not apply.

(v)   The ballot
- Voting must be by the voter marking a voting paper.
- Each voting paper must
  - state the name of the independent scrutineer where one is required
  - specify
    - the date by which; and
    - the address to which the voting paper is to be returned
  - specify who is authorised to call upon members to take the industrial action if the vote is in favour of industrial action
  - be marked with a unique number which is part of a consecutive series of numbers used for the ballot
  - contain at least one of the following questions:
    - a question which requires the voter, by answering 'Yes' or 'No', to say whether he is prepared to take part or in a strike
    - a question which requires the voter, by answering 'Yes' or 'No', to say whether he is prepared to take part or in industrial action short of a strike
  - contain the following statement (without qualification or comment):

    'If you take part in a strike or other industrial action, you may be in breach of your contract of employment.'

- Each person entitled to vote must
  - have a voting paper sent to him at his home or other mailing address
  - be given an opportunity to vote by post
  - be allowed to vote without interference from the union or any of its members, officials or employees; and
  - so far as is practicable be able to vote without incurring any cost to himself.
- A ballot must be conducted so that
  - so far as is practicable the voter can vote in secret; and
  - the votes in the ballot are fairly and accurately counted.
- As soon as is reasonably practicable the union must ensure that those who were entitled to vote and their employers are informed of the numbers of:
  - votes cast
  - individuals answering 'Yes' to the question or to each question
  - individuals answering 'No' to the question or to each question
  - spoiled voting papers.
(vi) Calling industrial action
- For industrial action to have the support of a ballot it must:
  - be called by the person specified on the voting paper as having authority to call it

- there must not have been any call to take the action before the date of the ballot; and
- the industrial action must take place within four weeks beginning with the date of the ballot. Where a court prohibits or suspends the taking of industrial action for any time then the union can apply to the court to extend the period so it has a full, unconstrained, four weeks in which to take industrial action.

- For industrial action to be protected the union must also ensure that the employer of anyone who will be called upon to take industrial action receives a notice of the action. This notice must not be given before the results of the ballot have been sent to voting members and must be received by the employer in question at least seven days before the industrial action referred to in the notice begins.

- The notice must:
  - identify the employees who are going to be called to take industrial action
  - state whether the action is intended to be continuous or discontinuous (ie whether once it starts it will take place on all the employees' working days or not) and
    - if continuous state the intended date when any employees will start to take part
    - if discontinuous state the dates when any employees will partake in the action
  - state that the notice is given for purposes of s 234A TULRA.

(d) *Action by an individual where goods or services are disrupted*

This provision was a major amendment to the law brought into effect by TURERA

(i)   The right

- Where, because of unlawful industrial action, whether actual or threatened, the supply of goods or services to an individual will or could be delayed or prevented or the individual would not be able to get the same standard of goods or services that individual may apply to a court. This applies whether or not the individual has a right to be supplied with those goods or services. Unlawful industrial action for these purposes is action: which is actionable in tort by one or more persons; or which would entitle an individual trade union member to take action against the trade union in question (*see 'Rights of trade union members against the union', 102.8 above*). Where a court finds an action well founded it can grant an injunction/interdict to restrain further action being taken.

(ii)   Assistance for individuals

- An individual who is an actual or prospective party to proceedings of the above type may apply to the Commissioner for Protection Against

Unlawful Industrial Action for assistance with bringing or pursuing a claim.
- In deciding whether and to what extent to grant an application for assistance, the Commissioner can take into account, amongst other things:
    - whether, in view of the complexity of a case, it is unreasonable to expect the applicant to deal with it unaided, and
    - whether the Commissioner considers the case involves a matter of substantial public interest or concern.

(e) *Dismissal of an employee whilst taking part in industrial action*
    These provisions have been amended slightly by TURERA.
    (i) Dismissal of those taking part in unofficial industrial action
    - An employee has no right to claim unfair dismissal if at the time of dismissal he was taking part in unofficial industrial action.
    - By an amendment brought in by TURERA this exclusion does not apply if the reason, or primary reason for dismissal or for selection for redundancy was:
        - to do with maternity
        - to do with being a health and safety representative or safety committee member or taking action in a health and safety case; or
        - to do with being an employee representative.
    - A strike will *not* be unofficial for these purposes if:
        - the person concerned is a trade union member and the action has been endorsed by his union
        - the person concerned is not a trade union member, but some of the people taking action are trade union members and the action has been endorsed by their union; or
        - none of the people taking part in the strike are trade union members.
    - Note that for these purposes:
        - if an employee is a member of a trade union which is not connected to his employment this is to be disregarded; conversely if he was a member of a union when the action began, but thereafter ceased to be one, then he is deemed to have continued to be a union member
        - where an employee is dismissed with notice the date of dismissal is the date when notice of dismissal is given
        - where the union repudiates any industrial action that repudiation does not take effect to make the strike unofficial until the end of the next working day after the repudiation.
    (ii) Dismissal of those taking part in official industrial action
    - An industrial tribunal cannot determine the fairness or unfairness of an employee's dismissal if at the date of dismissal
        - the employer was conducting or instituting a lock-out; or
        - the complainant was taking part in strike or other industrial action
        unless one or more employees who were also involved in the industrial

action or strike or were directly interested in the dispute giving rise to the lock-out ('relevant employees')
- has not been dismissed; or
- has been offered re-engagement within three months of his dismissal when the complainant has not.
- By an amendment brought in by TURERA this restriction does not apply if the reason, or primary reason for dismissal or for selection for redundancy was:
  - to do with maternity
  - to do with being a health and safety representative or safety committee member or taking action in a health and safety case; or
  - to do with being an employee representative.
- A complaint under this heading must be brought within six months from the date of the complainant's dismissal or, if that is not reasonably practicable, within such further time as is reasonably practicable.
- Where the complaint is of discriminatory re-engagement then the principal reason for dismissal for purposes of the ERA unfair dismissal/unfair selection for redundancy provisions and for purposes of dismissal/selection for redundancy for trade union reasons under TULRA is the reason for which the complainant was not offered re-engagement.

(f) *Criminal charges arising out of industrial action*
  (i) Breach of contract involving injury to persons or property
    - A person commits a criminal offence, punishable by a fine, if he wilfully breaches his employment contract knowing or believing that the probable cease of doing so (whether alone or with others) will be
      - to endanger life
      - to cause serious bodily injury; or
      - to expose real or personal property to destruction or serious injury.
  (ii) Intimidation or annoyance by violence or otherwise
    - A person (the intimidator) commits a criminal offence, punishable by a fine, if to make another do or abstain from doing something which that person is legally entitled to chose to do or not to do (as they wish), the intimidator
      - uses violence to or intimidates that person or his wife or children, or injures his property
      - persistently follows that person about from place to place
      - hides any tools, clothes or other property owned or used by that person, or deprives him of or hinders him in the use thereof
      - watches or besets the house or other place where that person resides, works, carries on business or happens to be, or the approach to any such house or place; or
      - follows that person with two or more persons in a disorderly manner in or through any street or road.
  (iii) Restrictions on the offence of conspiracy

- In England and Wales
  - where an act which amounts to a criminal conspiracy which:
    - is done in contemplation or furtherance of a trade dispute; and
    - is a summary offence, not punishable with imprisonment
  then it is not to be treated as a criminal conspiracy for purposes of prosecuting it as such.
- In Scotland
  - an agreement or combination by two or more persons to do or procure to be done an act in contemplation or furtherance of a trade dispute is not indictable as a conspiracy if that act committed by one person would not be punishable by imprisonment
  - where a person is found guilty of an offence which is punishable only on summary conviction, the maximum sentence is to be no more than three months or the statutory maximum which would apply if the offence had been committed by one person.

103 Trade Union and Labour Relations Acts 1974 and 1976

Originally the parts of these Acts relating to individual rights were repealed and consolidated into the Employment Protection (Consolidation) Act 1978. The Acts were further amended by the Employment Acts 1980 and 1982 with regard to collective matters (which were their only remaining sphere of operation). These provisions, as amended were consolidated into the TULRA.

104 Trade Union Reform and Employment Rights Act 1993 (TURERA)

This Act amended the Employment Protection (Consolidation) Act 1978, Transfer of Undertakings (Protection of Employment) Regulations 1981, Employment Acts 1980, 1982 and 1989 and the Trade Union and Labour Relations (Consolidation) Act 1992. The amendments to the EPCA have now been consolidated into the Industrial Tribunals Act 1996 and the Employment Rights Act 1996. The provisions of this Act are examined under the statutes into which they have been consolidated or which they amend.

105 Transfer of Undertakings (Protection of Employment) Regulations 1981

Amended by TURERA and by Collective Redundancies and Transfer of Undertakings (Protection of Employment) (Amendment) Regulations SI 1995/2587.

The Regulations were originally restricted to dealing with cases where a business, or part of a business, which was in the nature of a commercial venture was transferred from one person to another. This restriction, limiting the application of the Regulations to cases where the undertaking transferred was in the nature of a commercial venture, was removed by TURERA to bring the Regulations into line with the EC Directive which they were introduced to implement. This means that the transfer of any undertaking is now covered by the Regulations provided only that the undertaking was situated in the United Kingdom before the transfer and that the subject matter of the transfer is an 'undertaking' within this wider definition. TURERA further widens the ambit of what can amount to an undertaking by providing that no property need be passed from the transferor to the transferee for there to be a transfer under the Regulations. This makes it clear that the Regulations can cover the contracting-out of services by both commercial and non-commercial bodies – including government departments and local authorities – as well as the types of transaction which might more traditionally be viewed as a transfer of an undertaking. The major provisions of these Regulations are as follows:

105.1   Before the transfer

(a) *Consultation*

Originally the Regulations only required employers to consult where they recognised independent trades unions. The Collective Redundancies and Transfer of Undertakings (Protection of Employment) (Amendment) Regulations SI 1995/2587 now require consultation whether or not an independent trade union is recognised. Consultation is required in respect of all those employees who will be affected by the transfer. NB 'Employees affected' by the transfer are any employees in either the transferor undertaking (ie the seller), or the transferee undertaking (ie the buyer), who will be affected by the transfer. This does not merely apply to employees who will actually be transferred with the business.

(b) *Representatives for consultation*

- Where there is a recognised independent trade union then the employer can choose to consult either representatives of that union or employee representatives. If no independent union is recognised then the employer must consult employee representatives.
- The employer may consult employee representatives who either
  - have been elected by employees specifically to be consulted by their employer about the proposed transfer; or
  - were elected by employees for other purposes and who are considered appropriate (having regard to the purposes for which they were elected) for the employer to consult about the proposed transfer.

  They must also have been employed by the employer at the time when they were elected.
- If
  - the employer invites any of the employees who may be affected by the transfer to elect employee representatives; and
  - the invitation is made sufficiently far in advance of the time when the employer is required to give employee representatives information about the transfer, to allow for employee representatives to be elected in time to receive that information (*as to the information to be given see (c) below*)

then the employer is deemed to have complied with his statutory obligation to provide the information if he provides it as soon as is reasonably practicable after the representatives are elected.
- An employer must allow employee representatives:
  - access to the employees whom it is proposed to make redundant; and
  - accommodation and such other facilities as may be appropriate.

(c) *Information to be given to employee representatives*
- Long enough before the transfer for consultations to take place, the employer must inform the employee representatives of:
  - the fact of the transfer and the reasons for it
  - the legal, economic and social implications of the transfer for the affected employees
  - the measures which he envisages taking with regard to those employees in connection with the transfer; and
  - if he is the transferor, any measures the transferee envisages taking (a duty is placed on the transferee to provide the necessary information in this respect).
- Where an employer envisages that he will be taking measures in connection with the transfer he must consult with employee representatives about these. TURERA modified the consultation required about measures to be taken in connection with transfer, so that the employer must now seek in these consultations to obtain agreement to the measures to be taken.

(d) *Compensation for failure to consult*
- If an employer fails to consult, an award can be made against him by an industrial tribunal. The amount of the award will depend on the seriousness of the employer's failure and is subject to a maximum of four weeks' pay for each employee in respect of whom consultation should have taken place and did not. (TURERA amended the original provision which set the maximum award at two weeks' pay.)
- The appropriate claimant where an employer has not fulfilled the consultation requirements depends on the employer's particular failure. Where an employer has failed:
  - to fulfil any requirement relating to an employee representative the claim is made by the employee representative
  - to fulfil any requirement relating to a trade union representative the claim is made by the trade union
  - in any other case, the claim will be made by an employee who is affected by the transfer.

  A claim must be brought within three months of the completion of the transfer (or if that is not reasonably practicable within such further period as it reasonably practicable).
- If the transferor claims that he has failed to provide information about the measures the transferee intended to take after the transfer because the transferee failed to provide him with that information then:

- he must notify the transferee of this claim; and
- the transferee will then automatically be joined to the proceedings.

105.2   On transfer

(a) *Transfer of contracts*

The transferred employees' contracts are transferred with them and take effect as if they had been entered into with the transferee employer from the outset. The employees cannot leave and claim constructive dismissal unless either:

(i)   the change of ownership is a significant, detrimental, change for that employee; or

(ii)   the employee's conditions of work are substantially changed to his detriment.

By a TURERA amendment, however, an employee can leave when the undertaking is transferred simply because he objects to becoming an employee of the transferee's. But if he does this he will not be treated as having been dismissed by either the transferor or the transferee.

(b) *Occupational pension schemes*

Occupational pension schemes are expressly excluded from transfer under these provisions. TURERA has amended this provision to make it clear that this restriction is confined strictly to pensions *per se*. If there are benefits within the pension scheme which are not themselves to do with 'old age, invalidity or survivors' then they are not to be treated as part of the pension scheme and would need to be preserved by the transferee.

(c) *Transfer of liability*

- All the transferor's civil liability to, or in connection with, the transferred employees is also transferred to the transferee, except in a case where the employee elects, 'on a whim', not to be transferred to the transferee (*see (a) above*).
- Criminal liability is specifically excluded from being transferred but this would not prevent the transferee from becoming criminally liable immediately after the transfer for any offences which are continuing – such as continuing breaches of health and safety requirements.

(d) *Trade unions and collective agreements*

- Where an independent trade union was recognised before the transfer and the part of the business transferred maintains a separate identity, then union recognition is transferred for that part of the business.
- Any collective agreement pertaining to a transferred employee is also transferred.

105.3   Unfair dismissal and redundancy

(a) It is *prima facie* automatically unfair to dismiss an employee because of a transfer unless there are economic, technical or organisational reasons entailing a change in the workforce in either transferor or transferee workforce. If there is such a reason, and that reason entails a change in the workforce, then the employer is treated as having a substantial reason for dismissal. The tribunal is then required, in terms of s 98(4) Employment Rights Act 1996, to decide whether or not the dismissal was fair. If the dismissal was fair then the employee will usually be entitled to a redundancy payment.

(b) If the employee leaves voluntarily upon transfer then, unless he can show that there has been a substantial change in his terms and conditions of employment which is to his detriment, he will not be entitled to a redundancy payment because he will not have been dismissed.

106   Truck Acts 1831–1940

Repealed by Wages Act 1986 which has itself been repealed and consolidated into the ERA.

Provided that all persons in manual employment (except domestic employees) be paid in 'coin of the realm'. This restriction was lifted by the Wages Act 1986. The Truck Acts also contained restrictions on deductions which might be made from the wages of such employees. These restrictions were amended and extended to all employees by the Wages Act 1986 and are now incorporated into the ERA.

107   Unfair Contract Terms Act 1977

Has relevance for employers who want to limit their liability to employees. Section 2 of the Act states:

(a) a person cannot, by reference to any contract terms or to a notice given to persons generally or to particular persons, exclude or restrict his liability for death or personal injury resulting from negligence;

(b) in the case of other loss or damage a person cannot so exclude or restrict his liability for negligence except in so far as the term or notice satisfies the requirement of reasonableness;

(c) where a term of a contract or a notice purports to exclude or restrict liability for negligence, a person's awareness of the term or notice is not of itself to be taken as indicating his voluntary acceptance of any risk.

108   Wages Act 1986

Repeals Truck Acts 1831–1940, Payment of Wages Act 1960 and Wages Council Act 1979.

Amends Employment Protection (Consolidation) Act 1978.

Amended by Social Security Act 1986, Redundancy Rebates rights repealed by Employment Act 1989. The parts relating to Wages Council were repealed by Trade Union Reform and Employment Rights Act 1993.

The provisions re. deductions from wages and payments by employees to employers were repealed and consolidated into Employment Rights Act 1996.

108.1   Payment in 'coin of the realm'

The Wages Act 1986 repeals the Truck Acts' provisions insofar as they required that manual employees were paid in coin of the realm. Where employees have a contractual right to be paid in cash the Payment of Wages Act 1960 (also repealed by the Wages Act 1986) allowed for employees to opt for payment otherwise than in cash. However, any such agreement could be revoked by the employee on giving four weeks' notice. The effect of the repeals brought about by the Wages Act 1986 is that an agreement for non-cash payment is now irrevocable.

108.2   Deductions from wages/payments to employers

These provisions have been consolidated into the Employment Rights Act 1996.

108.3   Wages Councils

The Wages Act 1986 repeals the Wages Councils Act 1979 and significantly reduced the functions and powers of the Wages Councils. Wages Councils were finally abolished by TURERA with effect from 30 August 1993.

108.4   Redundancy rebates

The Wages Act 1986 reduced the availability of redundancy rebates so that only small employers could still claim them. The Employment Act 1989 removed the last vestiges of the right to claim redundancy rebates.

109   Wages Council Act 1979

Re-enacted the Wages Council Act 1959 as amended. This Act was repealed by the Wages Act 1986.

110   Workplace Health, Safety and Welfare Regulations (SI 1992 No. 3004)

This is one of the 'Six-pack' Regulations introduced in 1992 arising from European health and safety directives. The Regulations amend Shops and Railway Premises Act 1963 and Factories Act 1961.

These Regulations are concerned with the premises provided for employees to work in and with the fixtures, fittings and services, such as heating ventilation, sanitary facilities, etc. which are part of those premises. The requirements under these regulations include:

(a) *Ventilation*

Adequate ventilation must be provided. Where adequate ventilation is maintained by a machine which, if it broke down, would create a health and safety risk, an audible or visible alarm must be fitted to the machine to signal any breakdown.

(b) *Temperature*

The temperature in a workplace must be reasonable during working hours and an adequate number of thermometers must be provided to enable people to know what the temperature in the workplace is.

(c) *Lighting*

The lighting in a workplace must be suitable and sufficient and, so far as is reasonably practicable, should be natural light. Where there would be special hazards in a workplace if the lighting were to fail then emergency lighting must be provided.

(d) *Cleanliness*

The furniture and fittings in a workplace must be kept clean and waste must not be allowed to accumulate in the workplace (other than in suitable receptacles).

(e) *Working space*

There should be approximately 11 cubic metres of room space per person; although this may need to be increased if furniture or other fittings take up a lot of space in the workplace.

(f) *Work station*

(i)   Every workstation must be:
- adequately protected from bad weather
- designed to ensure that the employee/s can leave quickly, or be assisted away in the case of an emergency
- designed to ensure that the person working there will not slip or fall.

(ii)   Where work can or must be done sitting down then a suitable seat, and where necessary a suitable footrest, should be provided.

(g) *Floors and traffic routes*

(i)   Floors and traffic routes
- must be suitably constructed for the purpose for which they are used
- must not have holes in or be slippery or uneven.

(ii)   The workplace must be organised so that pedestrians and vehicles can circulate in a safe manner.

(iii)   Escalators and moving walkways must:
- function safely
- be equipped with necessary safety devices
- be fitted with an easily identifiable, easily accessible, emergency stop control.

(h) *Windows and doors*

(i)   Windows and other translucent materials in walls and doors must be made of safety material to prevent breakage and should be marked to ensure that people realise that the material is there.

(ii)   Windows and skylights which can be opened must not be in a position such that opening them could give rise to a health and safety hazard.

(iii)   All windows and skylights must be designed or constructed so that they can be cleaned safely.

(iv)   Doors and gates must be suitably constructed and have any necessary safety devices in particular:
- sliding doors must have a device to prevent them coming off their tracks; and

- upward opening doors must have a device to prevent them falling down.

(i) *Falling and falling material*

There must be adequate protection against employees falling or being struck by falling objects. Particular care must be taken to prevent employees from falling into or being struck by any dangerous substance (ie one which might burn or scald or which is poisonous, suffocating or corrosive or which by its mere volume is likely to cause danger if it escapes). Adequate protection may include fencing or covering dangerous materials and making adequate safety provision where work is being carried out on ladders or scaffolds or where materials are stored high up. The protection envisaged by this Regulation is *not* the provision of personal protective equipment, training or information about the danger unless no other protection is possible.

(j) *Sanitary conveniences, washing facilities and changing facilities*

   (i) An adequate number of sanitary conveniences and washing facilities must be provided
   - where the number of employees is less than five, then only one WC and one washing facility need be provided
   - a second WC and washing facility are required when the number reaches 25; and
   - an extra WC and washing facility should be provided for each additional 25 employees thereafter.

   (ii) Showers may also be required by the nature of the work.

   (iii) Washing facilities must have hot and cold or warm water available.

   (iv) Where employees change into different clothes for work, adequate facilities must be made available:
   - to keep clothes secure
   - to separate work and personal clothes where this is necessary in health and safety terms; and
   - to allow clothes to be dried where possible.

   (v) Where employees need to change into different clothes for work, adequate changing facilities must be made available for them.

(k) *Facilities for rest, eating meals and drinking water*

   (i) Suitable and sufficient rest facilities must be provided:
   - where necessary for health and safety
   - in which to eat food if:
     - food would otherwise become contaminated when eaten at work; or
     - where food is regularly eaten at the workplace.
   - Rest areas must have suitable arrangements to protect non-smokers from tobacco smoke.
   - Suitable rest facilities must be provided for pregnant women and nursing mothers.

   (ii) There must be an adequate supply of drinking water which is readily accessible to employees.

111   Young Persons (Employment) Acts 1938 and 1964

Repealed by the Employment Act 1990.

Part 3
Recommended Reading

The following titles provide a general introduction to employment law and to the law in particular subject fields. IPD members requiring recommended reading on specific items of legislation mentioned in this checklist or photocopies of case law are invited to apply to the IPD's Information and Advisory Services.

General

BOWERS, JOHN. *Employment Law*. 4th edn. London, Blackstone, 1997. lxxii, 533pp.

BOWERS, JOHN *and* HONEYBALL, SIMON. *Textbook on Employment Law*. 4th edn. London, Blackstone, 1996. lviii, 442pp.

CHANDLER, PETER. *An A–Z of Employment Law: A complete reference source for managers*. London, Kogan Page, 1995. xvii, 608pp.

DEAKIN, SIMON *and* MORRIS, GILLIAN S. *Labour Law*. London, Butterworth, 1995. liv, 920pp.

HOLLAND, JAMES A. *and* BURNETT, STUART A. *Employment Law*. 4th edn. London, Blackstone, 1997. xxiv, 321pp.

INCOMES DATA SERVICES. *Employment Rights Act 1996*. London, Incomes Data Services, 1996. 77pp (Employment law supplements 77).

KIBLING, THOMAS *and* LEWIS, TAMARA. *Employment Law: An adviser's handbook*. 2nd edn. London, Legal Action Group, 1996. xxxix, 334pp.

LEWIS, DAVID. *Essentials of Employment Law*. 5th edn. London, Institute of Personnel and Development, 1997. xxxvii, 314pp.

LOCKTON, DEBORAH J. *Employment Law*. London, Cavendish, 1996. xxvii, 308pp.

MOONEERAM, JUDITH, RICE-BIRCHALL, SIMON *and* WHITTERS, BERNADETTE. *Employment Law*. Bristol, Jordans, 1997. xx, [4], 179pp.

PAINTER, RICHARD W., HOLMES, ANN E.M. *and* MIGDAL, STEPHEN D. *Cases and Materials on Employment Law*. London, Blackstone, 1995. xxxviii, 672pp.

PITT, GWYNETH. *Employment Law*. 2nd edn. London, Sweet and Maxwell, 1995. lxii, 393pp.

SELWYN, NORMAN M. *Law of Employment*. 9th edn. London, Butterworth, 1996. lxviii, 767pp.

SLADE, ELIZABETH A. *Tolley's Employment Handbook*. 10th edn. Croydon, Tolley, 1996. lxviii, 567pp.

SMITH, I. T. *and* THOMAS, GARETH. *Industrial Law*. 6th edn. London, Butterworth, 1996. lxxii, 709pp.

WALLINGTON, PETER. *Butterworths Employment Law Handbook*. 7th edn. London, Butterworth, 1996. xiv, 1689pp.

WAUD, CHRISTOPHER. *The Daily Telegraph Employment Law 1995: The practical guide for personnel managers, trade union officials, employers, employees, and lawyers*. 11th edn. London, Kogan Page, 1995. 352pp. [12th edn due October 1997].

WHINCUP, MICHAEL. *Modern Employment Law: A guide to job security and safety*. 9th edn. Oxford, Butterworth Heinemann, 1997. lxi, 376pp.

Encyclopaedia

HARVEY, R.J. (ed). *Industrial Relations and Employment Law*. London, Butterworth. 4 vols. [Looseleaf, regularly updated].

UPEX, ROBERT (ed). *Encyclopedia of Employment Law*. London, Sweet and Maxwell *and* Edinburgh, W. Green and Son. 4 vols. [Looseleaf, regularly updated] [formerly Hepple & O'Higgins. *Encyclopaedia of labour relations law*].

Case Law Reports

INCOMES DATA SERVICES. *Employment Law Cases*. London, IDS. 11 vols (Looseleaf, regularly updated: Contracts of employment; Employment protection; Industrial tribunal and EAT procedure; Race and sex discrimination/equal pay; Redundancy; Trade unions; Unfair dismissal).

INDUSTRIAL CASE REPORTS. London, The Incorporated Council of Law Reporting for England and Wales, 1973–. (10 issues a year with annual bound volume).

INDUSTRIAL RELATIONS LAW REPORTS. London, Industrial Relations Services, 1972–. (monthly).

Journals

(see also under subject sections below)

EMPLOYMENT DIGEST. Kingston-upon-Thames, Croner (2 issues a month).

IDS BRIEF. London, Incomes Data Services (2 issues a month).

INDUSTRIAL LAW JOURNAL. London, Oxford University Press for the Industrial Law Society (Quarterly).

INDUSTRIAL RELATIONS LEGAL INFORMATION BULLETIN. London, Industrial Relations Services (2 issues a month).

TOLLEY'S EMPLOYMENT LAW & PRACTICE. Croydon, Tolley (Quarterly).

Wages

CONFEDERATION OF BRITISH INDUSTRY. *Cashless Pay and Deductions from Pay: A practical guide to the Wages Act 1986*. London, Confederation of British Industry, 1987. 39pp.

INCOMES DATA SERVICES. *Wages*. London, Incomes Data Services, 1996. ii, 132pp (Employment law handbooks, series 2, no. 11).

INCOMES DATA SERVICES. *Wages Act 1986*. London, Incomes Data Services, 1986. 28pp. (Brief. Employment law supplements 48).

SUTER ERICH *and* LONG, PHIL. *Cashless Pay and Deductions: Implications of the Wages Act 1986*. London, Institute of Personnel Management, 1987. vii, 95pp.

Company Law

GOWER, L.C.B. *Principles of Modern Company Law*. 5th rev. edn. London, Sweet and Maxwell, 1992.

Contracts of Employment

AIKIN, OLGA. *Contracts.* 2nd edn. London, Institute of Personnel and Development, 1997. xii, 251pp (Law and employment).

FORSTER, PETER. *How to Write and Understand Contracts of Employment.* London, Gee, 1995. v, 168pp (Employment in action).

LEIGHTON, PATRICIA E. *and* O'DONNELL, AIDAN. *The New Employment Contract: Using employment contracts effectively.* London, Nicholas Brealey, 1995. viii, 253pp (Law at work).

JULYAN, ALAN J. *Key Employee: Drafting service contracts.* 7th edn. London, FT Law and Tax, 1995. xxix, 305pp (Practitioners series).

WALTON, F. *and* CHAMBERLAIN, S. (eds) *The Employment Contracts Handbook: Practical guidance and procedures.* London, Gee, 1991. [Looseleaf, regularly updated.]

Data Protection

DATA PROTECTION REGISTRAR. *Data Protection Act 1984.* 2nd edn. Wilmslow, Office of the Data Protection Registrar, 1992 (Guidelines).
    1 Introduction to the Act. 19pp.
    2 The Definitions. 38pp.
    3 The Register and Registration. 31pp.
    4 The Data Protection Principles. 29pp.
    5 Individuals Rights. 29pp.
    6 The Exemptions. 39pp.
    7 Enforcement and Appeals. 23pp.
    8 Summary for Computer Bureaux. 8pp.

EVANS, ALASTAIR. *The Data Protection Act: A guide for personnel managers.* London, Institute of Personnel Management, 1984. v, 66pp.

INCOMES DATA SERVICES. *Employee Data.* London, Incomes Data Services, 1994. 37pp. (Employment law supplements 70).

INSTITUTE OF PERSONNEL AND DEVELOPMENT. *The IPD Guide on Employee Data.* London, Institute of Personnel and Development, 1995. 8pp.

Dismissal

BOWERS, JOHN. *Termination of Employment.* 3rd edn. London, FT Law and Tax, 1995. ix, 99pp (Practice notes).

JAY, LYNDA *and* PATCHETT, BOB. *Croner's Guide to Managing Redundancy.* Kingston-upon-Thames, Croner, 1995. vi, 170pp.

INCOMES DATA SERVICES. *Redundancy.* London, Incomes Data Services, 1996. ii, 205pp (Employment law handbooks, series 2, no. 10).

INCOMES DATA SERVICES. *Unfair Dismissal.* London, Incomes Data Services, 1993. 313pp (Employment law handbooks, series 2, no. 1).

RICH, MICHAEL A., MEAD, HELEN *and* EDWARDS, IAN. *Mead's Unfair Dismissal.* 5th rev. edn. London, Longman, 1994. iii, 415pp.

RUBENSTEIN, MICHAEL *and* FROST, YVONNE. *Unfair Dismissal: A guide to relevant case law*. 15th edn. London, Eclipse, 1997. [7], 105pp.

Employee Involvement

INCOMES DATA SERVICES. *Information and Consultation Rights*. London, Incomes Data Services, 1996. 77pp (Employment law supplements 75).

BOURN, COLIN *and* WHITMORE, JOHN. *Anti-Discrimination Law in Britain*. London, Sweet and Maxwell, 1996. xl, 345pp.

CLARKE, LINDA. *Discrimination*. 2nd edn. London, Institute of Personnel and Development, 1995. viii, 150pp (Law and employment).

ENGINEERING EMPLOYERS' FEDERATION. *Harassment at Work: The law*. London, Engineering Employers Federation, 1996. 70pp.

EQUAL OPPORTUNITIES COMMISSION. *Towards Equality: A casebook of decisions on sex discrimination and equal pay*. Manchester, Equal Opportunities Commission, 1995. xxvi, 349pp.

HEMMING, JULIAN, MASON, KATE *and* FISHER, DAVID. *Discrimination in the Workplace: A practical guide*. Chichester, Wiley, 1997. xxviii, 328pp.

HOUGHTON-JAMES, HAZEL. *Sexual Harassment*. London, Cavendish, 1995. xviii, 228pp.

INCOMES DATA SERVICES. *Bullying and Harassment at Work*. London, Incomes Data Services, 1996. 50pp (Employment law supplements 76).

INCOMES DATA SERVICES. *Race Discrimination*. London, Incomes Data Services, 1996. i, 128pp (Employment law handbooks, series 2, no. 9).

NICHOLLS, PAUL *and* BALL, PAUL. *Tolley's Discrimination Law Handbook*. 2nd edn. Croydon, Tolley, 1995. xxi, 361pp.

RUBENSTEIN, MICHAEL. *Discrimination: A guide to the relevant case law on race and sex discrimination and equal pay*. 10th edn. London, Eclipse, 1997. [7], 110pp.

UPEX, ROBERT *and* SHRUBSALL, VIVIEN. *Discrimination in Employment: Law and practice*. London, FT Law and Tax, 1995. xxv, 229pp.

WILLIAMS, AUDREY M. *Croner's Guide to Discrimination*. Kingston-upon-Thames, Croner, 1995. vi, 165pp.

Disability Discrimination

BRADING, JEAN *and* CURTIS, JOHN. *Disability Discrimination: A practical guide to the new law*. London, Kogan Page, 1996. 187pp.

CHELLIAH, RAMANI *and* LOCAL GOVERNMENT INFORMATION UNIT. *The Disability Discrimination Act 1995: A guide for local authorities*. London, Local Government Information Unit, 1996. 44pp.

DEPARTMENT FOR EDUCATION AND EMPLOYMENT. *Code of Practice for the Elimination of Discrimination in the Field of Employment against Disabled Persons or Persons Who Have Had a Disability*. London, HMSO, 1996. 58pp, x, [10].

DOYLE, BRIAN JOHN. *Disability Discrimination: Law and practice*. Bristol, Jordan, 1996. xliii, 496pp.

GARDINER, JO. *The Disability Discrimination Act 1995: Putting the law into practice.*
London, Industrial Society, 1997. viii, 96pp.

GOODING, CAROLINE. *Blackstone's Guide to the Disability Discrimination Act 1995.*
London, Blackstone, 1996. ix, 138pp.

INCOMES DATA SERVICES. *Disability Discrimination Act 1995.* London, Incomes Data
Services, 1996. 93pp (Employment law supplements 78).

O'DEMPSEY, DECLAN *and* SHORT, ANDREW. *Disability Discrimination: The law and
practice.* London, FT Law and Tax 1996. xlvii, 373pp (Law and tax practitioner).

THOMAS, GARETH. *The New Law of Disability Discrimination.* London, Sweet and
Maxwell, 1997. xvii, 200pp.

Equal Pay

EQUAL OPPORTUNITIES COMMISSION. *Code of Practice on Equal Pay.* Manchester,
Equal Opportunities Commission, 1997. 21pp.

INCOMES DATA SERVICES. *Equal Pay.* London, Incomes Data Services, 1994. 85pp
(Employment law handbooks, series 2, no. 3).

PACI, PIERELLA *and* JOSHI, HEATHER. *Wage Differentials between Men and Women:
Evidence from cohort studies.* Sheffield, Department for Education and
Employment, 1996. 111pp (Research series 71).

Health and Safety

AKASS, RON. *What Every Manager Needs to Know about Health and Safety.*
Aldershot, Gower, 1995. xv, 272pp.

BARRETT, BRENDA *and* HOWELLS, RICHARD. *Cases and Materials on Occupational
Health and Safety Law.* London, Cavendish, 1995. xx, 414pp.

BARRETT, BRENDA *and* HOWELLS, RICHARD. *Occupational Health and Safety Law.* 3rd
edn. London, M & E, 1997. xix, 299pp.

CHANDLER, PETER. *An A–Z of Health and Safety Law: A complete reference source for
managers.* London, Kogan Page, 1995. xvii, 636pp.

COX, SUE, JANES, BILL, WALKER, DEBORAH *and* WENHAM, DAVID. *Tolley's Office Health
and Safety Handbook.* Croydon, Tolley, 1995. xv, 260pp.

EARNSHAW, JILL *and* COOPER, CARY L. *Stress and Employer Liability.* London, Institute
of Personnel and Development, 1996. ix, 156pp (Law and employment).

GOODMAN, M.J. (ed) *Encyclopedia of Health and Safety at Work: Law and practice.*
London, Sweet and Maxwell *and* Edinburgh, W. Green and Son. 4 vols
[Looseleaf, regularly updated].

HEALTH AND SAFETY COMMISSION. *General COSHH ACOP (Control of substances hazardous to health) and carcinogens ACAP (Control of carcinogenic substances) and
biological agents ACOP (Control of biological agents): Control of substances hazardous to health regulations 1994: Approved codes of practice.* London, HMSO,
1995. vi, 74pp.

HEALTH AND SAFETY EXECUTIVE. *COSHH 1994: Approved codes of practice: A money-
saver's guide.* Sudbury, HSE Books, 1995. 11pp.

HEALTH AND SAFETY EXECUTIVE. *A Guide to the Reporting of Injuries, Diseases and Dangerous Occurrences Regulations 1995 [RIDDOR]*. London, HMSO, 1996. vi, 84pp.

HEALTH AND SAFETY INFORMATION BULLETIN. London, Industrial Relations Services (monthly).

HENDY, JOHN (ed) *and* FORD, MICHAEL. *Redgrave, Fife and Machin: Health and Safety*. 2nd edn. London, Butterworth, 1993. lxxxviii, 2429pp.

KING, BRIAN, LEWIS, PAUL *and* BATEMAN, MIKE. *The Handbook of Health and Safety at Work*. London, Kogan Page, 1996. 694pp.

MUNKMAN, JOHN, HENDY, JOHN *and* FORD, MICHAEL. *Munkman on Employer's Liability*. 12th edn. London, Butterworth, 1995. cxiii, 573pp.

ROTH, ELISABETH *and* NICHOLAS, KATHARINE. *Occupational Illness*. London, Longman, 1995. xvii, 194pp.

STRANKS, JEREMY. *Health and Safety Law*. 2nd edn. London, Pitman, 1996. viii, 263pp.

WICKERSHAM, CAROLE. *Croner's Guide to Health and Safety*. 3rd edn. Kingston-upon-Thames, Croner, 1995. v, 170pp.

Industrial Relations and Trade Unions

BARROW, CHARLES. *Industrial Relations Law*. London, Cavendish, 1997. xxxvii, 370pp.

BOWERS, JOHN, BROWN, DAMIAN *and* GIBBONS, STEPHEN. *Trade Union Reform and Employment Rights Act 1993: A practical guide*. London, Longman, 1993. xxvii, 352pp.

CONFEDERATION OF BRITISH INDUSTRY. *A Hard Act to Follow? CBI Guide to the Trade Union Reform and Employment Rights Act 1993*. London, Confederation of British Industry, 1993. 41pp.

DU-FEU, VIVIAN, WARREN, MARTIN *and* WILLIAMS, AUDREY. *Collective Labour Law: A guide to the rights and obligations of employers, trade unions and employees*. London, Croner, 1992. 100pp.

ENGINEERING EMPLOYERS' FEDERATION. *The Trade Union Reform and Employment Rights Act 1993: An employers' guide*. London, Engineering Employers' Federation, 1993. 40pp.

INCOMES DATA SERVICES. *Industrial Action*. London, Incomes Data Services, 1995. ii, 166pp (Employment law handbooks, series 2, no. 7).

INCOMES DATA SERVICES. *Trade Union Reform and Employment Rights Act 1993*. London, Incomes Data Services, 1993. 65pp, [1] (Brief. Employment law supplements 68).

INCOMES DATA SERVICES. *Trade Unions*. London, Incomes Data Services, 1997. ii, 184pp (Employment law handbooks, series 2, no. 12).

MORRIS, GILLIAN S. *and* ARCHER, TIMOTHY J. *Trade Unions, Employers and the Law*. 2nd edn. London, Butterworth, 1993. ix, 334pp.

Industrial Tribunals and Employment Appeal Tribunals

GREENHALGH, ROGER M. *Industrial Tribunals.* 2nd edn. London, Institute of Personnel and Development, 1995. viii, 188pp.

INCOMES DATA SERVICES. *Challenging and Enforcing Tribunal Decisions.* London, Incomes Data Services, 1995. 114pp (Employment law handbooks, series 2, no. 6).

INCOMES DATA SERVICES. *Industrial Tribunal Practice and Procedure.* London, Incomes Data Services, 1994. iii, 288pp (Employment law handbooks, series 2, no. 4).

MCMULLEN, JEREMY *and* EADY, JENNIFER. *Employment Tribunal Procedure: A users' guide to tribunals and appeals.* London, Legal Action Group, 1996. xl, 413pp.

PETTINGER, RICHARD. *Preparing and Handling Industrial Tribunal Cases: A practical guide.* Hitchin, Technical Communications, 1995. vii, 62pp (Busy manager: best practice management reports).

Pensions

DAWES, HARRIET *and* SAMSWORTH, JANE. *Guide to the Pensions Act 1995.* London, Financial Times, 1995. xxxiii, 404pp.

FENTON, JONATHAN, HAM, ROBERT *and* SABEL, JOHN. *Tolley's Pensions Handbook.* 2nd edn. Croydon, Tolley, 1995. xxxii, 720pp.

IDS PENSIONS SERVICE BULLETIN. London, Incomes Data Services (monthly).

INGLIS-JONES, N. *The Law of Occupational Pension Schemes.* London, Sweet and Maxwell. 2 vols. [Looseleaf, regularly updated.]

INSTITUTE OF PERSONNEL AND DEVELOPMENT. *The IPD Guide on Trusteeship and the Pension Act 1995.* London, Institute of Personnel and Development, 1996. 38pp.

OCCUPATIONAL PENSIONS. London, Industrial Relations Services (monthly).

REARDON, ANTHONY M. *Allied Dunbar Pensions Handbook.* 6th edn. London, Pitman, 1997. x, 388pp.

SELF, ROGER. *Croner's Guide to Pensions.* Kingston-upon-Thames, Croner, 1996. vi, 224pp.

WARD, SUE. *Managing the Pensions Revolution: A practical guide to pension schemes.* London, Nicholas Brealey, 1995. x, 278pp (Law at work).

Redundancy

ENGINEERING EMPLOYERS' FEDERATION. *An Employers' Guide to the 1995 Regulations about Consultation over Collective Redundancies and Business Transfers.* London, Engineering Employers' Federation, 1996. 16pp.

FOWLER, ALAN. *Redundancy.* London, Institute of Personnel Management, 1993. x, 198pp (Law and employment).

INCOMES DATA SERVICES. *Redundancy.* London, Incomes Data Services, 1996. ii, 205pp (Employment law handbooks, series 2, no. 10).

INSTITUTE OF PERSONNEL AND DEVELOPMENT. *The IPD Guide on Redundancy.* London, Institute of Personnel and Development, 1996. 14pp.

JAY, LYNDA *and* PATCHETT, BOB. *Croner's Guide to Managing Redundancy*. Kingston-upon-Thames, Croner, 1995. vi, 170pp.

LEWIS, PAUL. *The Successful Management of Redundancy*. Oxford, Blackwell, 1993. xviii, 197pp.

ROTHWELL, TIM *and* LOCAL GOVERNMENT MANAGEMENT BOARD. *Compensation, Severance and Redundancy Payments: Practitioner's pack*. London, Local Government Management Board, 1995. 53pp.

Social Security

LABOUR RESEARCH DEPARTMENT. *State Benefits 1997: A guide for trade unionists*. London, Labour Research Department, 1997. 56pp.

MATTHEWMAN, JIM, et al. *Tolley's Social Security and State Benefits 1996–97*. Croydon, Tolley, 1996. xiv, 743pp.

Statutory Maternity Pay and Statutory Sick Pay

CONTRIBUTIONS AGENCY. *Statutory Sick Pay: Manual for employers*. London, Department of Social Security, 1995. 70pp.

COWELL, EMMA, KORN, ANTHONY *and* NICHOLLS, PAUL. *Croner's Guide to Pregnancy, SMP and Maternity Rights*. 2nd edn. Kingston-upon-Thames, Croner, 1994. 156pp.

COX, SUSAN. *Maternity Rights*. London, Industrial Relations Services, 1996. i, 186pp.

DURRANT, ALEXANDRA *and* DINEEN, SUSAN. *Operating SSP and SMP*. London, Gee, 1994. xv, 176pp.

INCOMES DATA SERVICES. *Maternity Rights*. London, Incomes Data Services, 1994. iii, 164pp (Employment law handbooks, series 2, no. 5).

LABOUR RESEARCH DEPARTMENT. *Maternity Rights: An LRD guide to the law and best practice*. London, Labour Research Department, 1997. 48pp.

MORRIS, SUE. *Statutory Maternity Pay and Maternity Rights*. London, Industrial Society, 1995. vi, 125pp (Employment matters).

PALMER, CAMILLA. *Maternity Rights*. London, Legal Action Group, 1996. xxxv, 292pp.

SELF, ROGER. *Tolley's Employment and Maternity Benefits*. 3rd edn. Croydon, Tolley, 1994. xxvii, 324pp.

Taxation

INCOMES DATA SERVICES. *The Personnel Manager's Tax Guide, 1996/97*. London, Incomes Data Services, 1996. 79pp (Research file 38).

INLAND REVENUE. *Expenses and Benefits: A tax guide*. London, Inland Revenue, 1995. 80pp.

MAAS, ROBERT W. *Tolley's Taxation of Employments*. 4th edn. Croydon, Tolley, 1995. xxxix, 396pp.

TAXATION. London, Taxation Publishing Co. (weekly).

Transfer of Undertakings

ENGINEERING EMPLOYERS' FEDERATION. *Business Transfers: The law and how to apply it in practice*. London, Engineering Employers' Federation, 1995. 93pp.

INCOMES DATA SERVICES. *Transfer of Undertakings*. London, Incomes Data Services, 1995. i, 167pp (Employment law handbooks, series 2, no. 8).

LOCAL GOVERNMENT MANAGEMENT BOARD. *CCT, Pensions and Transfers: An information guide for local authorities*. London, Local Government Management Board, 1995. 39pp.

LOCAL GOVERNMENT MANAGEMENT BOARD. Employment Advice Unit. *CCT, TUPE and the ARD: Legal and practical implications: An information guide for local authorities*. London, Local Government Management Board, 1996. 70pp.

MCMULLEN, JOHN. *Business Transfers and Employee Rights*. 2nd edn. London, Butterworth, 1992. xxxix, 320pp.

INDEX